Theatre for Young Audiences

edited by
Nellie McCaslin

The Program in Educational Theatre
The School of Education
New York University

Longman
New York and London

Theatre for Young Audiences

Longman Inc., New York

Associated companies, branches, and representatives throughout the world.

Copyright © 1978 by Longman Inc.

Developmental Editor: Gordon T. R. Anderson
Editorial and Design Supervisor: Nicole Benevento
Design: Pencils Portfolio, Inc.
Manufacturing and Production Supervisor: Louis Gaber
Composition: Fuller Typesetting of Lancaster
Printing and Binding: The Maple Press Company

Library of Congress Cataloging in Publication Data

Main entry under title:

Theatre for young audiences.

   Bibliography: p.
   Includes index.
   1. Children's plays—Presentation, etc.—Addresses, essays, lectures. I. McCaslin, Nellie.
PN3157.T4   792'.0226   77-17710
ISBN 0-582-28011-7

Manufactured in the United States of America

Contents

V SELECTED BIBLIOGRAPHY

Foreword

It is a privilege to be accorded the first opportunity to comment on the essays in this volume. They comprise a collection of singular importance to the developing field of theatre for young audiences—a field much in need of articulate accounts of the working philosophies and evolving aesthetics of several of its leading practitioners. Perhaps the adult theatre can draw on dicta from ages past to explicate, define, and illuminate its efforts; but that particular brand of the art now called theatre for young audiences has a heritage by the grandest stretch less than two hundred years old and, for all practical purposes, a heritage of only seventy-five years. Small wonder we need to turn to contemporary, practicing artists and educators in our profession to formulate a growing aesthetic, one that can be amplified and modified by succeeding generations of practitioners and theorists.

It is to Dr. McCaslin's credit that she has succeeded in collecting and offering to the field this thoroughly varied series of perspectives on theatre arts as applied to children and youth. This volume, together with her earlier *Children and Drama* on the subject of creative drama with children, provides a striking record of the advances made since the publication of *Children's Theatre and Creative Dramatics,* a 1961 volume edited by Geraldine Siks and Hazel Dunnington. The two McCaslin volumes need to be studied together because, as several of the contributors point out, the trend toward blending theatre arts and creative drama is one distinct development of recent years.

As one reads through these articles one is struck with the vitality and creative energy of the writers. No stodgy tomes, these! Herein lie statements of commitment and resolve, guided by belief in an important mission and informed by extensive experience and careful study. Such a variety of ideas and ways to approach the art form! Who are those who accuse this field of cliquishness and one-mindedness, with everyone adhering slavishly to precepts originally articulated in the 1930s by sainted pioneers? Surely if what guides us today did indeed come from such pioneers, then they have done their work well. For were all these writers to appear simultaneously in the same room I wager we would hear the rumble and see the fur fly across the breadth of the land, signaling a healthy competition of ideas.

For example, after reading these chapters, imagine if you will the discussion on participation theatre between Brian Way and Marjorie Sigley on

one side, with Mary Jane Evans and Orlin Corey on the other. Or stand by
neutrally (if you can) while Thomas Kartak holds off Judith Liss on the
subject of developing a single recognizable style of children's-theatre production. No doubt direct conflict of expression was not elicited in compil-
ing these essays, but the inclusion of directly contradictory ideas on these
and other subjects will make for uniquely stimulating reading.

One group of these essays highlights the working philosophies of several
exemplary theatre programs. Judith Liss explains the background and
production methods of the famous Paper Bag Players of New York.
Thomas Kartak gives a detailed account of the Nashville Children's
Theatre and Academy's system of combining production with a drama
school. John Clark Donahue gives an intriguing explanation of the unique
methods and concepts evolved by the Children's Theatre Company of the
Minneapolis Institute of Fine Arts, wisely cautioning that they "may not
travel well" to other theatres. Two well-known organizations in the
U.S.S.R. share billing in this group. Natalya Sats, founder of the movement
in Russia, writes clearly and simply about her job as regisseur of the Moscow Lyric Theatre for Children; and Zenovi Korogodsky provides us with
an unusual look into the principles governing the Leningrad TIUZ under
his direction. Brian Way provides a welcome account of his historic work at
the London Theatre Centre in developing the genre of participation
theatre, while Marjorie Sigley writes almost lyrically about her background
as educator and theatre artist as it led inevitably to her founding the Young
People's Theatre of New York.

Fortunately all of these writers express concern for broad questions, not
merely giving a narrow view of their own theatres' operations. Attention to
matters of age-group appropriateness, acting methods and training,
theatre's relation to film and television, indeed to many questions of broad
application make these chapters in some respects mini courses in children's-theatre production and design.

Several authors stress our responsibilities to the profession. Orlin Corey,
well known for his poetic writing as well as speaking style, reminds us of
our charge to pass on intact and unadulterated the myths of the race to the
next generation, avoiding any tendency to sacrifice to the spurious gods of
relevance any universal truths our material may contain. Mary Jane Evans
charges us to be cautious about blind service to the gods of experimentation, especially gratuitous participation, at the possible sacrifice of lasting
values. By contrast, Brian Way, in advocating participation theatre, stresses
the need for the right producing conditions if one is to expect success.

Eloquent appeals to expand our concepts of audience and broaden our
age-group focus into a family-interest theatre are made by John Clark
Donahue, Orlin Corey, Judith Liss, Kelsey Collie, Zenovi Korogodsky,

Brian Way, and Grigore Pogonat. Thomas Kartak reminds us again of the need for continued efforts to establish graded sequences of theatre-arts experiences for every child; and the Romanian, Grigore Pogonat, calls once more for extensive audience research in our unique "laboratory theatres." Patricia Snyder, in recounting the story of her uniquely funded state-supported Empire State Youth Theatre, focuses on the whole matter of the public and private sectors' responsibility in supporting such programs across the country—an appeal echoed by Marjorie Sigley while recounting the financial woes of her organization at New York's Civic Center.

As always, beautifully articulate, succinct and challenging, Sara Spencer gives in her chapter a perspective of children's-theatre playwriting since 1904, telling us in her inimitable way not be be too discouraged nor yet too smug about what progress has been made. Kelsey Collie traces the development of theatre for black children in the United States, ending with a timely appeal for plays explicating black life-styles. Richard Courtney carefully evolves an aesthetic that provides a needed rationale for both conventional and participatory theatre forms.

The very fact that one may with validity compare remarks made continents apart speaks of a vast change in our perspectives in the past ten or twelve years. McCaslin has recognized the growing internationalism of the field and has wisely included articles by highly visible and respected artists from abroad and placed them cheek by jowl with those of their American colleagues. Though not all the ASSITEJ countries are represented here, we have opportunity to juxtapose perspectives from Canada, England, Romania, the U.S.S.R., and the United States. And, it must be pointed out, international comparisons are not merely academic exercises. Through the workings of ASSITEJ, which McCaslin explains in her Introduction, such comparisons have become actual through international congresses, festivals, and demonstrations.

Readers will be stimulated to compare and contrast these writers' words and ideas. The authors attest collectively to a wide range of "rightness" in production. They provide a critical look at where we have been and some directions we may go. They maintain a healthy perspective, wearing neither rose-colored glasses nor cloaks of doom. They bespeak a growing maturity of the profession they serve.

Read, enjoy (or fume), think.

Jed H. Davis, University of Kansas

Preface

When *Children and Drama* was published in 1975, a number of readers suggested that it be followed by a book on children and theatre. By theatre they meant the theatre as an art form in which the child is the spectator rather than the participant. Generally speaking, although at the present time there is some conscious blending of forms, participation and spectatorship are separate and distinct experiences, each desirable but differing in their objectives and values. I was delighted with the suggestion; indeed, I had already considered writing a book on the subject. But with the positive reaction to the format of *Children and Drama,* it was obvious to me that there would be greater value in the viewpoints of a number of well-known contributors than there would be in the opinions of any single writer.

Just as *Children and Drama* presents the philosophy and, in some cases, the methodology of a group of leading educators, so this new book includes a variety of opinions on what constitutes good theatre for young audiences as expressed by well-known and influential producers and directors of theater for young audiences. Through a study of their philosophies and practices the reader is able to see the major directions that children's theatre is taking today. That, in essence, is what *Theatre for Young Audiences* is all about. Its *raison d'être* is the current interest in a subject about which there are enthusiasm and dissatisfaction in almost equal measure.

This answers the *what* and the *why* of the book. A much more difficult question to resolve was *who* should speak to the subject. Despite the acknowledged mediocrity of much that passes for children's theatre today, there are some men and women both in the United States and abroad who are doing splendid work; they are serious practitioners with high standards, clear and consistent points of view, distinctive styles of their own, and an acknowledged influence over others. Some of these directors/producers are to be found in the educational field, some in the community theatre, and some in the professional or commercial sector. In an anthology of this kind it seems both fair and more representative to include leaders from each of these three areas. Television and film are excluded from consideration because the focus of the book is on the living theatre. Puppetry, though qualifying as live entertainment, is a different art form and therefore not included.

My search for a variety of viewpoints among well-known persons in the field of children's theatre eventually led me to the names listed in the table of contents. The majority are American. Those representing England,

Canada, Russia, and Romania were included because of our familiarity with their work and the influence they have exerted on theatre for children in the United States. Brian Way, for example, has conducted workshops here, and his participation plays are well known. The work of Richard Courtney is as familiar to many of us as it is to his colleagues in Canada. Natalya Sats, founder of children's theatre in Russia and director of the Central Moscow Children's Musical Theatre, was the keynote speaker at the convention of the Children's Theatre Association of America in New York in 1973; and the Romanian director, Grigore Pogonat, opened the 1976 convention in Los Angeles. Zenovi Korogodsky directs one of the most exciting theatres for young spectators in the world. Children's theatre enthusiasts, traveling in Russia, always return stimulated by performances seen at his Leningrad TUIZ (Theatre for Young Spectators). There are other directors in both the United States and Europe whose work elicits high praise from visitors, but the limitations of space prohibit the inclusion of more than fifteen contributors.

In addition to the well-known companies, for example, there are a number of relatively new groups doing excellent and innovative work. Among them are The Looking Glass Theatre of Providence, Rhode Island, a professional company working closely with the schools in the area. Not yet four years old is the Creative Arts Team of New York University's Program in Educational Theatre. This is an American theatre-in-education team of actor-teachers who research, develop, and perform their own material based on topics of current interest. The Magic Carpet, a San Francisco-based company of young actors, has developed a still different format in which stories written by children are solicited and used as scripts. There are other groups too numerous to mention, but these three companies are cited because they are illustrative of some of the new directions being taken and the high quality of work that is emerging in many places.

I was delighted by the enthusiasm of those to whom I wrote and grateful for their cooperation. I must also express appreciation to those persons originally consulted as to the format of the book and possible contributors. Of particular value were the thoughtful suggestions made by Lowell Swortzell of New York University. My gratitude also goes to Miriam Morton for her translations from the Russian.

Theatre for Young Audiences is a frank and penetrating look at children's theatre today: how the writers conceive of it and why; what it is and what it can become. Perhaps this collection of essays by people who are deeply concerned as well as actively engaged in creating theatre for children will do more than inform; it may even affect the future course of theatre for young people in this country and, as a consequence, theatre for adults as well.

                                                                    NELLIE McCASLIN

Introduction

In the preface a rationale was offered for yet another book on children's theatre. That rationale appeared more valid to me with each manuscript I received. I realize now that this anthology is much more than a presentation of current thought on the subject; it is also an exploration of social attitudes and human needs in this last quarter of the twentieth century. As adults concerned with the performing arts, we cannot help viewing them on two levels: current theatre practices for the young and the prospects for adult audiences of the future.

If there is one area of the American theatre that has managed to survive neglect and malnutrition, it is children's theatre. From its beginning in the first decade of this century to the present day, children's theatre has been beloved but not respected, praised but denied professional recognition, approved but not supported. It has been said that love is necessary to survival. If that is true, perhaps love has been the secret of its tenuous hold on life. Without love, children's theatre would surely have withered and died, except for the drama the children themselves created. Theatre for children in our century was founded on the belief in its power to entertain, teach, inspire, and bring human beings together. It has been nurtured for these reasons, but it has now passed from the hands of the amateurs to those of the professional teachers, actors, and community-theatre directors. It is time that it be given proper status.

When we stop to consider what is available to the average young spectator in America and the place assigned to theatre in our society, we have cause for discouragement. Theatre, an art form that has entertained and inspired humankind for more than two thousand years, is today a threatened species. Of course, this cry has been heard before, but the circumstances in which the theatre is expected to exist have changed radically in the past thirty-five years. The lack of any form of living theatre in many parts of the country, the soaring costs of production and the price of tickets where it does exist, and the widespread acceptance of television as an adequate means of entertainment have relegated the living theatre to a position on the periphery of our lives—too frequently a luxury to be enjoyed by an elitist audience, if and when it is available. The average adult has little opportunity to enjoy the performing arts, and there are many young people who attend their first plays in college, either as field trips or attendance at university productions. There are exceptions, certainly, but I doubt that anyone in our country today would claim the theatre to be

1

central to the life of his or her community and therefore vital to the social, intellectual, and emotional well-being of the people who live in it. The direction that the American theatre takes in the next quarter century will be up to our children and young people. Their response to its beauty and their faith in its power to explore human nature and the problems of society will largely determine the extent and quality of its growth. Their regard for it, however, will depend on their exposure. What experience with theatre have they had? As participants? As spectators? What are they likely to have in the future? Or will they settle for television without ever having discovered what the living theatre has to offer?

HISTORICAL BACKGROUND

Before venturing an answer to any of these questions, let us take a look at the history of children's theatre in this country—where it came from, who founded the first programs and why, and where these programs were located. Let us examine the objectives that guided them, the leadership that emerged as programs were developed, the forms that these programs took. Perhaps then we can see the present in its proper perspective. It may even help us to plan for the future, a future in which theatre will be a significant and integral part of our lives.

The date ascribed to the beginning of children's theatre in the United States was the year 1903. Its birthplace was the Educational Alliance in New York City, a settlement house on Manhattan's lower East Side. The founder, Alice Minnie Herts, was a social worker with a background in theatre and a strong belief in its educational and socializing powers. Her reasons for founding the Children's Educational Theatre were threefold: to bring the people of the ghetto better entertainment than was available locally; to help teach a new language to the children of the immigrants; and to meet the pressing social needs of the neighborhood. The project was a great success from all three standpoints. Unfortunately, finances, always the plague of children's theatre, forced the suspension of activities in 1909. Meanwhile, the idea had caught on, and the next decade was to see the beginnings of dramatic activities for children in other settlement houses in New York, Chicago, and Boston. The years before and after World War I brought a rash of amateur productions, dramatic classes, and story hours from coast to coast, with support coming largely from recreation departments, community centers, civic theatres, Junior Leagues, and the American Drama League, a national organization founded in 1919. There was little interest in producing plays for children on the part of the professional theatre, though Clare Tree Major and Junior Programs, Inc. toured productions to hundreds of American cities during the Thirties and Forties.

The Federal Theatre of the Depression was the first government-subsidized theatre in this country, but though it was highly successful in many ways, it lasted only three years. Those three years, however, served more than the purpose for which it had been established—to give jobs to unemployed actors, writers, and technicians. The Federal Theatre for Children reached into communities that previously had never known live theatre. In addition, the Federal Theatre captured the interest of a number of writers and directors, who continued to work in this field after the project was officially terminated.

The Twenties and Thirties meanwhile were seeing the first of the "town-gown" operations. Evanston, Illinois, was an outstanding example of cooperation between a university and a board of education. Winifred Ward of Northwestern University's School of Speech was founder and first director of the Children's Theatre of Evanston. In making a distinction between children's theatre and creative dramatics, she also defined terms and clarified objectives. After the Second World War the leadership shifted from the communities to the schools and colleges, and educators began to replace social workers as leaders. In 1944 the first national professional organization, now known as the Children's Theatre Association of America, was formed. It was not until 1952, however, that this committee became a full-fledged division of its parent body, the American Educational Theatre Association. By this time productions for children were being given in all parts of the country by college and university drama departments, and descriptions of courses in creative dramatics and children's theatre were appearing in the academic catalogues.

In the meantime, drama continued to be a popular and well-supported activity in civic theatres and recreation centers. During the Fifties there was a spurt of activity in the commercial sector. Small professional companies, both resident and touring, sprang up on the East and West coasts. Again, money was a major problem, for without subsidy of some kind, the most highly acclaimed companies could not meet operating expenses, let alone employ Equity actors and build quality programs.

The Sixties, which saw a sharp drop in the number of these small professional groups, witnessed the first of the new government grants for arts programs. Support from private foundations, State Arts Councils, the National Endowment for the Arts, and Title I and Title III monies (the Elementary and Secondary Schools Arts) made possible some extensive programs throughout the United States and enabled some of these groups to expand their activities. The picture was still far from encouraging at the end of the decade, however, as these grants were not a permanent source of income. They were designed to aid the creation of new projects and were not intended to meet the running expenses of established programs, regardless of their quality. And so, while children's theatre was given a transfusion, it was not extended the kind of support that it needed in order to grow into a strong, ongoing institution.

STATUS OF THEATRE FOR CHILDREN TODAY

Where, then, is children's theatre today? This is a question to which there are many possible answers. Geographically speaking, children's theatre is to be found in all parts of the United States. It exists under the auspices of educational, community, and professional management. It is paid for by public and private funds, box-office receipts, and volunteer help. Despite subsidies and grants, better prepared performers, and professional organizations that are engaged in raising standards, children's theatre is still far from the dream that its founders had for it. On this one point we can get a consensus. Beyond that, opinions vary widely as to its quality and worth. What theatre for children could or should be depends, it seems, on the objectives and values of the respondent.

The greatest controversies center on scripts, style of production, length of performance, children as actors, and age grouping of the audience. Most producers and sponsors feel strongly about one or more of these points. And because there is so much difference of opinion, every type of producing group has its critics as well as its supporters. Personally, I find some work that I think remarkably good, more that I consider mediocre, and much that is inadequate by any standard. In my reactions I am referring primarily to script and production.

Some of the questions that seem to be of greatest concern to producers and sponsors of children's plays have to do with content, purpose, and style of presentation. If there is such a thing as appropriate subject matter, who should determine its suitability? Should children's plays be dramatizations of traditional stories treated traditionally? Or should they, on the other hand, have original plots based on modern material and contemporary themes? Are such plays more relevant to young audiences of today than the folk and fairy tales, the legends and the classics that have been the accepted fare in the past? Or should children's plays continue to use traditional material given modern treatment and a current thrust?

Closely related to content is purpose. Is the goal of children's theatre entertainment or is it education presented in an entertaining manner? What social values should be implanted in children's scripts, or should the theatre be used for this purpose? Should aesthetic values be the major consideration? What about the adolescent audience? Do we consider his/her interests, or is the high school student ready for adult plays?

As to style of production, which is more desirable—proscenium or arena? Should participatory drama replace conventional spectator theatre?

Is improvisation more effective than the scripted play? Is the musical enjoyed by young audiences more than the straight play? Are music and dance always a desirable addition, or do they detract when imposed to enliven sagging scenes? Will some of the innovations such as story theatre, short sketches on a single theme, and improvisations be lasting forms, or does their appeal lie in their novelty? Finally, should children's theatre imitate adult theatre, or is it a different genre, demanding different content, form, and style?

Some of the other controversial issues concern producing groups and the strengths and weaknesses of current offerings. There is the matter of who should produce plays for children's audiences: college and university groups, community players, or professional (commercial) companies. Is there a place for all of these, and does each have a special contribution? In many instances the professional company gives a technically superior performance, whereas a university group may have a greater sensitivity to its audience. The community theatre, on the other hand, with a cast of adults and children, may have an added dimension through bringing a community together in the best historical tradition.

A question is often asked concerning audience composition. Is an audience of children preferable to one that is mixed—adults and children together? What about age-level programming? Some producers have strong feelings about the makeup of the audience.

There are reactions regarding the place in which children's plays should be presented. Is a special building necessary? Is it desirable to have an auditorium designed for this purpose alone and used for no other? Or is the school stage or all-purpose room preferable because of its accessability and the opportunity it affords for tying in the production with the school day? Does its familiarity rob it of magic? Does street theatre, in eschewing all formal theatre convention, reach its audience more directly than drama experienced in an auditorium?

What do we as a people hold as values in theatre for children? Most successful producing groups state their values and goals, but how many of these are commonly accepted? Finally, there is one overriding question: Is, should, or can the theatre become an art form that is central to the lives of all children? When this happens, it seems to me that it will assume equal importance in the lives of adults.

EXPRESSED NEEDS
Scripts

The first need appears to be for workable, literary playscripts. We need more new plays based on contemporary themes, and we must encourage our best playwrights to write for young audiences. On the other hand, I should regret seeing the folk and fairy tales dropped from the repertories. This traditional material is an important part of our cultural heritage and still makes good drama in the hands of a skilled playwright. A season that provides nothing new, however, ignores the power of the theatre to explore human problems and stimulate thinking on social issues. I do not advocate the use of children's theatre for political ends, but neither do I approve the exclusion of the here-and-now. An artist is an interpreter of the times; should not the artist working in children's theatre also recognize and present the world that he/she perceives?

What I look for but rarely find in theatre for young people of any age is literature, free of condescension and presented with integrity, artistry, and intelligence. I am offended by the "spoof" and the "in joke" that attempt to appeal to both young and old by irrelevant and often vulgar humor. Even when this kind of thing is defended on the grounds that children enjoy it, I cannot accept it as honest work. It encourages laughter for the wrong reasons and, what is worse, cheats an audience that has come expecting something else. There must necessarily be selection of incidents when dramatizing stories, but the original intent of the author must be respected.

At the present time there are few good scripts with original plots available to the children's-theatre director. Furthermore, many of these scripts are weak in the very qualities that make for the strong, absorbing drama that the authors claim to be lacking in traditional material. I find a preponderance of the trivial that not only underestimates the child's ability to deal with the problems that concern him but also misses the opportunity to offer more substantial fare. Some light entertainment is certainly in order, but a diet of the trivial is, in the end, self-destructive. The audience eventually tires of it or, worse, does not learn that there can be something better.

This may be one of the reasons for the accepted short performance. Today's fifty-minute show implies the child's inability to remain absorbed for more than an hour at a time. Children have historically been able to sit through a two- or a two-and-a-half-hour play, and audiences of young people in Europe take the two-hour performance for granted. The forty-five-minute school assembly period, for which many productions are designed, certainly has much to do with today's standard performance. There is also the standard length of the television program that rarely exceeds an hour and is, moreover, divided into short segments by commercials. Whereas some television programs do offer superior entertainment and substantial content without commercials, the fact that they are viewed at home with its built-in distractions usually precludes the kind of involvement that live theatre has to offer.

Finally, there is the current trend on the part of some commercial producers to gear plays to a very young audience. This practice is fraught with danger. When material considered appropriate for children from seven to ten or eleven is watered down for preschoolers in an attempt to capture their attention, the older child, capable of a greater depth of meaning and a richer vocabulary, is bored and loses interest. The result is a return to the television screen in an attempt to find something more in tune to his or her interests.

Production

The script is not the only aspect of children's theatre that is open to criticism. Playhouses, acting, mounting, and dramatic criticism are all inadequate. While we do have a handful of playhouses built specifically for the presentation of children's plays, they are woefully few in proportion to the wealth and size of our country. In general, children's productions are given in adult theatres during off hours, in large high-school auditoriums, or in all-purpose rooms in community centers or elementary schools. Rarely are these areas adequate. The ideal auditorium for a children's play is small and attractive, with good visibility from all parts of the house, and excellent acoustics. A large coatroom off the lobby, where children may leave their wraps, is a splendid idea, for physical comfort adds immeasurably to the enjoyment of the occasion. Having a building of their own gives children pride of possession, and going to a special place adds another dimension to the occasion.

It has been said that the acting in children's theatre is inferior to that on the adult stage. This is generally true. One reason is the fact that children's-theatre companies rarely stay together long enough to develop ensemble work and a distinctive style of performance. Talented professional players move on to roles in adult theatre or television, and talented college students are graduated. Moses Goldberg lists in his book *Children's Theatre: A Philosophy and a Method* certain essentials for the actor: sincerity or avoidance of condescension, the ability to play to and with the audience, range, training in voice, mime, singing, and dance.[1] The actor in the adult play should be similarly prepared, but the actor for children finds himself/herself in a more active role and certainly in a more responsible position as to guiding the audience or helping it grow.

Mounting—scenery and costumes—is a particularly important element of the production for children; unfortunately, it is far too often carelessly assembled. Old scenery, left over from adult plays, and ill-fitting, sometimes dirty costumes are used in the apparent assumption that children do not know the difference and therefore it does not matter. "Dressing up" is

1. Moses Goldberg, *Children's Theatre: A Philosophy and a Method* (Englewood Cliffs, N.J.: Prentice-Hall, 1974), p. 157.

all that is required. This is not only an insult to the child in the audience but
a missed opportunity to cultivate the aesthetic and the intellectual. Goldberg states that the two functions of design in the theatre are narrative and
graphic.[2] Because of the child's dependence on the visual, he believes that
the director/designer relationship in children's theatre is much more important to success than is the director/playwright relationship. Whether
spectacle is demanded or whether the play calls merely for the suggestion
of time and locale, imagination is the basic ingredient. Children are respon-
sive to visual excitement and love sudden changes of setting, color, or light.
Because of their own lively imaginations they are also able to see a house in
a cardboard box or a complete costume in a hat or scarf, as the Paper Bag
Players of New York City have so admirably proved to us.

Criticism

The drama critic for children's theatre in the United States has been
conspicuously lacking from the beginning and for obvious reasons. Most of
the work has been amateur, and little of it has warranted professional
recognition. Occasionally a newspaper has covered a show, but when it has
done so it has generally been because of its social importance to the community rather than acceptance of its value as art.

SUMMARY

At the Festival of International Theatre for Young People held in Car-
diff, Wales, in July 1977 many of these same concerns and problems were
voiced. They included the validity of the concept of theatre for children;
age level programming; buildings vs. open spaces for the presentation of
plays; theatre-in-education or T.I.E. (at this point, primarily a British
movement); government subsidy for children's theatre; improvisation; necessity for young people's theatre "to explain itself"; public relations; content that is relevant to the lives of children today; standards; values; teaching through theatre; the need for variety; and, finally, "fun and
enjoyment" vs., or in addition to, "education."

The only difference between these questions and those that have been
asked over the past fifty years is quantitative, not qualitative; more persons
are concerned about more aspects of the subject and the communication is
far more extensive than it has ever been.

It has been stated that plays for children are presently being produced
under the auspices of educational, community, and commercial organizations. I believe that all three should continue to be involved, though I
should like to see the commercial or professional theatre establish and

2.   Ibid., p. 167.

maintain the artistic standards. Neither the community theatre, most of which is amateur, nor the college theatre, with its consistent turnover of student actors, can develop the ensemble and technical excellence of the professional company that devotes all of its time and creative energy to the job. Until there is sufficient subsidy, however, this cannot happen. At current ticket prices commercial children's theatre cannot pay for itself; at increased prices it cannot get an audience.

In summary, I believe lack of money to be the greatest deterrent to the growth and quality of theatre for young people in the United States. Of greater significance, however, is the reason for this lack, and that is the place accorded the serious artist in our society. Until we believe in the value of the arts in the lives of all human beings, we shall continue to give them minimal support, regarding them as a fringe benefit, peripheral to our basic interests and needs. Our attitude toward the arts for children is even less generous. Until we as a people embrace the arts in general and the theatre in particular, we will not get the necessary funds. Some progress has been made through arts councils and foundations, but we have a long way to go before we can say that children's theatre in America is a strong and significant force.

What I want to see in theatre for children and young people is an art form, created with respect and a caring concern. An art form that is technically as fine as that produced for adults. An art form that touches every level of human consciousness, though not necessarily at the same time or in equal measure. An art form that stretches the mind and stirs the emotions.

I want to see a theatre that invites identification with strong protagonists both male and female. One that stimulates the imagination as it opens new doors. A repertoire that is as varied as it is excellent. Good theatre must include the serious, the comic, the multi-ethnic, the everyday, and the spectacular. It should represent the old and the new and appear in different styles. Staging should embrace the proscenium and the arena.

This theatre of which I speak must no longer be housed in a basement or loft, unless it be experimental, nor can its tenancy continue on a sublet basis. It is high time that it possessed a home of its own, a residence befitting its station and function. In its auditorium must be produced the best plays in America, performed by well-trained and sensitive actors. This theatre must be available to all children, as are our public schools and libraries. It will take money, but if we believe in its worth, we will pay the price. When we are able to say that children's theatre exists in every city in the United States and is available to the children of every rural and suburban community, we will have more than a renovation; we will have a great art form with a foundation on which to build a strong adult theatre for the future.

The following words of John F. Kennedy describe our goal eloquently:

To further the appreciation of culture among all the people, to increase respect for the creative individual, to widen participation by all the processes and fulfillments of art—this is one of the most fascinating challenges of these days.

PART I
The Child Audience

Set for "The Master" by Maxim Gorky. Dramatized and directed by Zenovi Korogodsky for the Leningrad Theatre for Young Spectators.

Zenovi Yakovlevich Korogodsky was born in 1926 in Leningrad. He went to the Leningrad Theatre for Young Spectators (TIUZ) in 1962, after twelve years in the adult theatre, including the celebrated Academic Bol'-shoi Theatre named after Gorky—the leading professional company of Leningrad.

Korogodsky became artistic director of the TIUZ when this theatre experienced a letdown following the termination of a forty-year leadership by its founder, Aleksander Briantsev. The company was in need of fresh creative energy and innovation, both of which the new head soon supplied in impressive measure. His creative restlessness and ardent love of his profession—and of the young audiences it serves—have brought vitality, contemporaneity, and stimulating controversy not only to the Leningrad TIUZ but to the world of Soviet theatre for children and youth generally.

Zenovi Korogodsky has been awarded the title of Merited Leader in the Arts of the Russian Soviet Federated Socialist Republic (RSFSR). He has directed and produced some twenty-five plays since 1962 and has taken a leading responsibility for the functioning of the school for acting conducted by the TIUZ.

RESPECTING THE CHILD SPECTATOR[1]

1

ZENOVI KOROGODSKY
Translated by Miriam Morton[2]

The children's theatre differs from the adult theatre in the way that a childless family differs from a family with children. No sooner is a child born than the whole existence of the family changes. It experiences new concerns, new joys—in short, its entire life pattern becomes different from what it was. Similarly, the only factor that distinguishes youth theatre from the stage for grownups is the fact that the spectators are children. We ponder how to offer the child what is most essential to him. How do we talk to him and about what? What may be permitted and what restricted? What, we wonder, are his interests today, and what will he clamor for tomorrow? And, generally, we are aware of how complicated and difficult it is to penetrate into his world—the inner world of childhood!

What sets apart the artist of the children's theatre is his feeling for contemporary childhood. The artistic level of his work depends on the depth and fullness of this feeling.

When theatres for young spectators were being established in our country, their enthusiasts were filled with a profound love and a sense of responsibility for the spiritual welfare of the children of the newborn republic—the first socialist land in the world. In those early years Aleksander Briantsev[3] wrote: ". . . the future leaders of the TIUZs [Theatres for Young Spectators] must feel the greatest devotion to the theatre and its audience."

1. This essay is translated from the journal, *Teatr*, July, 1971. Moscow: Ministry of Culture of the U.S.S.R.
2. See footnote 2 on p. 109.
3. Aleksander A. Briantsev was the founder, in 1922, of the Leningrad Theatre for Young Spectators. For the next forty years, he was its artistic director and leading spirit of the Soviet Theatre for Young Audiences.

When we speak seriously today about the greatest danger to our theatres for children and their artists, we must admit that this danger consists of our weakening concern for, and diminishing closeness to, the child spectator. Somehow the old feeling of genuine interest, the deep involvement with the upcoming generation, is absent. What has taken its place? Too often the children's-theatre practitioner sees his work as a routine assignment and merely seeks to get the job done. This is shown first of all in an indifference to discovering the *special interests of today's children.* It is a sort of functional deafness to the real, concrete demands and needs of today's boys and girls.

Not seldom does one hear the opinion that children are merely children and never mind probing any further. They always wanted such and such, they are capable of understanding only so much and not more, and we should talk to them only thus. Those preaching such an attitude do not want to, or cannot, see that children exist and are influenced by the current temper of the times, which is created by adults.

Today, children's awareness of the social environment evidences itself at a much earlier age, and this is to be expected. Our children live in a time when an enormous amount of new information is transforming the world. They react more vitally than we do, respond to all the exciting and threatening discoveries of our epoch, and being free from established points of view and false preconceptions, they are more searching than we adults. If it fails to acknowledge this characteristic of young beings, the children's theatre will not be essential to today's young audiences and consequently will not be able to fulfill its civic mission—to guide the development of the young citizen of our society.

It is for sound reasons that the problems of child guidance have become today a subject for widespread and varied discussion. All the errors we adults commit in our work with children arise from the attitude we take toward them. In the case of the theatre this is true in full measure. If the theatre as a collective upbringer of children considers them unchangeable, it becomes bit by bit (often unnoticed by itself) conservative, and thereby it not only alienates them but is even harmful to them.

Can we assume that the splendid play of our childhood, *The Red Kerchief,* will find a response from contemporary school children or *The Diploma* from teenagers? Of course not. And this does not in any way discredit the historical suitability of these fine productions in the children's theatre. It is simply that the times and the children have changed. It is obvious that not only the sense but even the staging devices (lighting, sets, costumes, and, most important, the style of acting) of these not so old theatrical accomplishments would not be received today as they were in their own time. This is the eternal and wonderful role of change. Is it something to worry about?

Nonetheless, it is still necessary to point out to many that childhood does not stand still. Unwillingness to recognize this and to understand contemporary childhood is tantamount to the absence of civic responsibility in the artist working with children. Can there exist a theatre for adults that does not understand its spectator and is not concerned about his interests? Yet how often in the children's theatre we exploit the defenselessness of children, their, so to speak, voicelessness (after all, they are not represented in any Departments of Culture, nor on the editorial boards of newspapers or magazines) or, more exactly, their tolerance. We offer them the first thing that becomes available or something that has become old and is no longer usable.

What is so wonderful about the child is his striving for adulthood. The child, the adolescent, wants to be not only a grownup but one of the better grownups. From this stems his real need for models to imitate. Therefore those who consider childhood unchangeable, subject to eternal verities or authoritative fiat and stereotypes, deprive them of something vital—their aspirations for the future, their quest for new knowledge, and their right to seek such knowledge themselves.

And is there not, tied to all this, an even more harmful tendency in the approach of adults to children that can be called a position of distrust? There are adults who agree that today's children are not the same as yesterday's, but they consider the contemporary children worse. At this point I should like to say categorically, yes, they are not the same children but nevertheless they are better than we think them to be. As far as I am concerned, I am certain that on the whole (assuming that we can talk about children as a "whole") they are better than we were in our time. All the insults—ignoramuses, nincompoops—complicate our guidance work with children.

Today's children are as different from the way we were as today's times differ from those in which we grew up. They know more today, they see more. They are freer and more open. Perhaps they are more difficult and less obedient than we were, but they live more richly and more interestingly than we did. This of course they owe to those adults who helped raise life to a higher level and created its new quality. To look at today's children through the eyes of our own childhood is pedagogical and even historical myopia.

We instill in the consciousness and soul of the child a certain set of moral and aesthetic norms—that is, we create the future. It is essential that a child be accepting of our influence. We cannot impose it or it will not become a part of his development. Taking account of his needs—this is the most important condition for influencing him. Yet, equally important is our confidence in our ability to guide him.

Here the most difficult problem of enlightenment arises, and it is not limited to art. Can we really speak to school children about everything? Our great educator, Anton Makarenko, gave to this question a definite and even categorical answer: "There is no subject with which we cannot trust children."

I happened to speak with a twelve-year-old schoolboy who had seen the film *Hamlet,* and not only did he understand the essence of the Shakespearean work but he was genuinely moved by the various filmic elements in the production and by the acting of the protagonist. This is not an isolated instance. We often encounter parents who bring their children to see a play that is not indicated for their age group. The parents declare, not without pride, "*Our* child will understand it." When I attend the theatre or a film with my own child I am also sure of his comprehension, of his brightness. Does not that mean that Makarenko is right? Are there no premature and too difficult themes for a given age? This would mean, then, that the confidence we must show in the children in this regard is without limit. Yet one hesitates to affirm this too readily. The personal response of a youngster differs intrinsically from his response when he is with his peer group—that is, when he is part of an audience of young spectators. Therefore the answer to the question Can we discuss *anything* with children from the stage? cannot be given unequivocally.

First of all, we must clarify what we mean by "anything." "Anything" means anything that the child can respond to from the vantage point of his experience, according to his emotional growth, and the general level of his development. In addition, in dramatic art the decisive factor is *how* to address the audience. In the TIUZs there are so-called forbidden themes. There were more of them in the past; now their number is decreasing. In the past, for example, it was impossible to show a negative adult character in the children's theatre, the exceptions being mainly Baba-Yaga and spies. Now the forbidden themes are mainly those that strongly excite the young spectator both sexually and in the area of social problems. In my opinion it is better to deal with such "forbidden" themes properly and in psychologically healthy terms than to let them remain a constant and increasing source of enticement or perplexity, thus at best leaving it to the child himself to solve these problems or at worst trusting the street or the playground to "discuss" them.

We must approach children seriously, but a serious approach to them, a respect for their feelings and aspirations, does not mean "maturing" the children's theatre so it approximates the adult theatre, something that some TIUZs have justly been accused of in recent years. The danger of such "maturing" is that it causes certain TIUZs to want to attract adult audiences rather than resulting in a greater respect and a more correct attitude toward the young spectator. These are two distinct approaches, and they must not be confused. For the pursuit of adult spectators is engendered by a lack of confidence in the young audience, whereas a serious approach to this audience entails, first of all, confidence.

"All of contemporary child guidance is motivated by the effort to make the child easy to live with . . . courteous, obedient, good, undisturbed, and hardly a thought is given to his thereby becoming inwardly unassertive and generally devitalized." (Janusz Korchak, *How to Love a Child.*)[4] A child need not be comfortable. We must develop in him creative powers. This the theatre can do if it does not chew over truths known to children from their primers, when it speaks to its audience as to equals, and poses questions that it answers together with the spectator.

It is about time to notice that children react not only to the subject and content revealed by the plot of a dramatic work but also to a great deal more than that—to the many elements that make theatre an art, such as the implications of the play's events, the metaphoric associations, the timing, the style of staging, the color and lighting. If the children did not show responsiveness to all this, then we could not regard theatre as a source of aesthetic education. The essence of aesthetic education is the indissoluble bond between the content and the aesthetic means of its dramatization. Therefore, when we assert that children are not capable of, or have not yet matured sufficiently for, aesthetic appreciation we often remain unresourceful, uninventive in marshaling the kinds of expressive means that serve to illumine, to make strongly impressive the moral values suggested in the content. But in fact the child, as Korchak has said, "surpasses us adults in the emotional forcefulness of which he is capable. . . ."

Lack of belief in the child and lack of respect for him generate in the theatre a wish merely to please, cater to, and indulge the child in the audience. Knowing how accepting and unsophisticated is our young spectator, we can imagine the aesthetic, professional, and civic level to which the theatre can sink. Disputes and polemics about the civic and cultural services of art are most sharply relevant to the children's theatre. Clearly, the core of art's humanistic service is the vital feeling—felt with pain and joy—the feeling for a better future and the struggle to assure it. The children's theatre is in the front line of this struggle.

Painful concern, deeply felt responsibility for children is the heart of the children's theatre. And there is enough reason for concern. Look around you. How many children's lives are made tragic by damaging family problems, wrong parental approach to childhood, traumatic mishandling of children, insensitivity, neglect! How can we of the children's theatre remain calm about this? The civic involvement of an artist is measured by his anxiety for the upbringing of the young citizen, who will determine the future of our society and, with other nations' young citizens, the future of our world.

4.   Janusz Korchak—a pediatrician and eminent Polish educator, children's playwright and author. During World War II he was the director of an orphanage. Its children were sent to the gas chambers. Although he himself was Jewish, the Nazis offered to spare him. But he insisted on being with his charges in their last moments and perished with them.

Richard Courtney is currently Professor of ——
Arts and Education at the Ontario Institute
for Studies in Education in Toronto. Prior to
this appointment he taught at the Universities of Victoria and Calgary and was a Senior
Lecturer in Drama in London. Professor
Courtney has also lectured and led workshops throughout the United Kingdom, the
United States, Europe, Australia, and Asia.

He was responsible for establishing Devel-
opmental Drama as a university discipline in
Canada. His writing includes, in addition to
articles in scholarly journals, *Play, Drama and
Thought: The Intellectual Background of Dra-
matic Education* (now in its third edition),
Teaching Drama, The School Play, and *The
Drama Studio.*

Richard Courtney is past president of the
Canadian Child and Youth Drama Association and the Canadian Conference of the
Arts. He is currently Chairman of the Task
Force on Arts and Education in Canada and a
board member of the Associated Councils of
the Arts (U.S.A.).

MAKING UP ONE'S MIND: AESTHETIC QUESTIONS ABOUT
2 CHILDREN AND THEATRE

RICHARD COURTNEY

INTRODUCTION

When we ask questions about the relationships of children and theatre we are not asking simple questions. The relationships are complex, and, although fundamentally philosophical and aesthetic, they impinge on broad areas of human study—psychology, sociology, and ethnology being among them. The relation of children to theatre is one instance of the general problems of existence. But it is an instance that is significant and important.

Throughout life we are continually occupied with our mental constructs. In each moment of existence we have a relationship with the external world. We activate the relationship, and, in that sense, we are constantly creating *who we are*. This also occurs in the playhouse but in particular ways.

At the same time, *who we are* colors our relationship to the world. Thus it affects our relationship to the arts and, specifically, students' relationship to theatre. This is the case whether they are percipient or creator, audience or actor. The relationship is contextual; or, as Brian Way says, "start from where you are."

"Making up one's mind" characterizes our dynamic with art and the student's dynamic with theatre. "Making up one's mind" is one of the activities of *who we are*. Yet, at the same time, it leads to the mental constructs whereby inner and outer coexist in our known reality.

This article will examine some aesthetic questions about the phenomenon of "making up one's mind" from the viewpoint of theatre and children.

MEANING

The relationship of children to theatre is always active and meaning-giving. This applies whether the student is watching a performance, is giving a performance, or is engaged in creative drama with no audience at all. Yet, in each instance there are differences in the meaning-giving operations of the students.

As a member of the audience the student interacts with the theatrical work of art. On the surface this may appear to occur in two extreme ways: passively, with presentational theatre, and actively, with participational forms. With presentational theatre (Barrie, say, or Chorpenning) we might falsely assume that the student is passive. Although he may not be physically active (unless he is bored) he is, nevertheless, actively imagining from the stimulus of the performance. So, even in this limited instance, it is difficult to say he is passive. With participational theatre (such as the plays of Brian Way, or the social "happenings" of Albert Hunt) the student is active both physically and imaginatively. The student actually joins in to create the artwork. But, surely, in presentational theatre too, the student *intends* the artwork and so helps create it?

Thus our initial distinction is insufficient. It may contain elements of truth, but it does not tell us enough of the situation.

Because students in theatre are always "making up their minds" and thus constantly giving meaning to the artistic experience, they are always active—whatever the style of the performance. Whether the form of theatre is presentational or participational, improvised or based on a text, spontaneous or rehearsed seems to make no difference. Children who are in a theatre experience provide it with meaning.

But what types of meaning?

THE STUDENT AS PERCIPIENT

In presentational theatre the student is a percipient; he is perceiving an artwork presented to him by others. What sort of meaning does the student give to this style of performance?

This type of theatre art form only exists when an audience is part of the event. I have shown elsewhere[1] that an audience *co-creates* the artwork of theatre. A rehearsal, perfect in every detail, can exist. Yet it is merely a work. A performance (which, of necessity, has the audience present) is an *artwork*. Any actor knows the difference between an audience that is "warm" or "cold." In each instance the art form is to some degree different because of the nature of that audience. Thus the student as percipient is contributing actively to the theatrical event.

Moreover, that theatrical event is *specifically designed* to include the contribution of the child. As a percipient in the playhouse, the student is an
inherent part of the work of art that is designed to include his activity. It is
so designed that he can "make up his own mind." Such a theatrical performance is made up of many elements—the actor, the ensemble, color,
light, shape, words—and each allows for the active contribution of the
student.

Let us take the example of the words, or script. A play script is so written
that the student's active presence is required. Robert Bolt's *The Thwarting
of Baron Bolligrew* may be the bones, the work of actors and director may be
the muscles, and the designer may provide the blood, but it is the corela-
tionship of all of these with the audience—the dynamics of the interchange
—that gives living flesh to the theatrical artwork.[2] By extension, we can see
that the student's mind gives every work of art its reality. By perceiving it,
the student joins the artist in his creativity. The student's consciousness is
not merely passive or reactive; it establishes a meaning-giving dynamic that
gives the theatrical work of art significance, even beyond the significance
envisaged by the artist.[3]

That the words are a mere skeleton of what the student apprehends is
most obviously seen in poetry. For example

My heart leaps up when I behold
A rainbow in the sky

is more skeletal than

So shalt thou feed on Death, that feeds on men,
And Death, once dead, there's no more dying then.

Although the theatrical situation may be more complicated, the words of
the script are no less skeletal but, as with poetry, in varying degrees. The
opening lines of James Reaney's "The Killdeer"

Oh no! I've never used cosmetics in my life
And I've certainly no intention of starting
Now

are more skeletal than

I can feel its damp sweet darkness
Brooding with frogs singing against my face.

The student reader "fills up" the poet's meaning, to a greater or lesser
degree depending on the directness of the work. The poet has written the

poem to allow for this "filling up" process. The meanings given by the student are possible in a number of dimensions, some of which are

(1) for themselves alone (e.g., music);
(2) for individual literal and symbolic meanings;
(3) for interrelationships between themselves into specific structures (which also have literal and symbolic meanings);
(4) for relationships between themselves and their creator (e.g., personal historicism); and
(5) for relationships between themselves and the percipient.

Moreover, at these and other levels there is a necessary ambiguity. The "filling up" of the reader may or may not correspond with the intention of the poet, though this often appears to be the case. A poem does not fulfill its function (e.g., it is not specifically an *artwork*) until this "filling up" takes place. Without this, it remains a work.

What occurs with poetry is similar to words in the playhouse, though there are differences largely due to complication. Students do not read the words but *hear them acted.* The words become multidimensional. Children hear them delivered by actors, who are directed by directors and placed in an aural and visual space by designers. Thus the student has further dimensions of "filling up" to achieve than with the reading of a poem. Put otherwise, the student's *intentional* activity is so much the greater.

It is the student's mental activity that allows his consciousness to provide the artwork with meaning. We can characterize the type of mental activity involved as imagination. I have elsewhere[4] put forward a theory of imagination that shows an active oscillation of mind. This is built on the energetic mechanism of identification and impersonation, swinging between inner and outer, the subjective and objective. In a genetic and developmental context, this energetic mechanism activates mind to relate to the environment by considering possibilities.

Yet it is play through which the child learns to utilize this mechanism. Play occurs when identification becomes externalized, and, as Winnicott has shown,[5] play is the way in which the child begins to relate inner and outer through "mediate objects." Through play we steadily build our relationship with the environment into our personal mental structures. Tagore said:

On the seashore of endless worlds
Children play.

This echoes, curiously, Sir Isaac Newton's

> I do not know what I may appear to the world, but to myself I seem to have been only a boy playing on the sea-shore, and diverting myself in now and then finding a smoother pebble or a prettier shell than ordinary, whilst the great ocean of truth lay all undiscovered before me.

Genetically considered, the child builds the "endless worlds" of play into the adult "world structures" of Alfred Schutz.[6] Even the adult is continually "making up one's mind": creating new structures whose oscillations permit him to relate to the work of art through possibilities.

The child as a member of an audience is faced by the theatrically alive form which he co-creates by contributing his mental activity. But it is not merely that the child provides the work with meaning. Also, the theatrical presentation becomes part of the "world structure" of the individual child. The performance (because the child is inherently part of it) becomes incorporated within the child's mental structures. It feeds and enriches his imaginative capacity, his potential for mental possibility. Piaget is fond of pointing out that, within mental structures, nothing is ever new; when the child incorporates a theatrical experience, he is providing all his later "world structures" with a richness and a fecundity that is ineffable. Whereas Sara Smilansky has shown the effect of lack of play on the socially disadvantaged child,[7] we can only guess at the deprivation that results from the lack of theatrical experience.

Children who can attend presentational and participational performances are greatly advantaged. Mentally, both categorical and spontaneous methods (both form and process) are jointly used within the oscillating mechanism. The variety of methods encourage the richness with which imagined possibility is so characterized.

Then, once the mind has chosen between the various splendors of possibility, the act becomes a value judgment about the work of art, the theatrical event. But it is a value judgment in which the student "makes up his own mind." It is unique to the specific consciousness, to the individual child. Thus it has its own forms of oscillation, its own emerging structures, its own individual images, patterns of imaging, and degrees of awareness.

In sum, the student's apprehension of presentational theatre provides it with meaning and so co-creates the work of art. Yet, at the same time, the student's own consciousness is enriched. By incorporating the performance, the child enriches the potential of his own mental structures in preparation for his adult "world structures." Moreoever, this permits him to develop the essential human freedom of a teleological value judgment.

THE STUDENT AS PARTICIPANT

Participational theatre for children provides wider contexts for meaning. Here the child is more obviously a creator. For example, in Brian Way's *The Mirror Man* the children are asked to act as if they are blowing magic dust (and similar activities) without which the play could not proceed. Participational theatre thus incorporates the *creativity* of the students directly.

However, creativity is a very complicated issue. Certain elements of it must be examined before we can proceed further.

Spontaneity

There appears to be a relationship between creativity and spontaneity. Moreno has said:

> Spontaneity operates in the present, *hic et nunc*. It propels the individual towards an adequate response to a new situation or a new response to an old situation. Thus, while creativity is related to the act itself, spontaneity is related to the warming up, to the *readiness* to act.[8]

I have examined elsewhere[9] the relationships of spontaneity to theatre as such, but, in terms of children, there appear to be three main levels of spontaneity (see as points on a continuum):

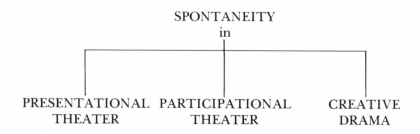

SPONTANEITY
in

PRESENTATIONAL   PARTICIPATIONAL   CREATIVE
THEATER   THEATER   DRAMA

In presentational theatre, spontaneity can only be in terms of mind. In participational theatre and creative drama, however, total spontaneity is encouraged; yet the type of spontaneity is limited by the activity. In both latter cases the student is given the *what?* but not the *how?* Even so, the nature of the *what?* varies. In participational theatre, *what?* questions must be in terms of the theatrical event; in creative drama, *what?* questions can be much wider and can have, if necessary, only tangential relationship to form. Thus, it is clear, greater spontaneity is permitted in creative drama;

yet participational theatre permits greater spontaneity than presentation. However, creative drama is not our concern in this essay, and this commentary will be confined to participational theatre.

Creativity

The term "creativity" is not mere "problem-solving," as some would have us believe. Gilchrist has indicated[10] that confusion has resulted from the application of the term "creativity" to different stages of the process of creative achievement. Normally the term may refer to a) the potential of the individual for such achievement; b) the intervening process by which the individual's behavior is directed toward a creative product; and c) the finished product itself. In some instances there may be a "problem," and in some instances there may be a "solving"—but both are not necessary at all times. Curiously, however, Gilchrist's three frames of reference relate closely to the levels of spontaneity open to children in drama/theatre experiences:

(a) the potential of the individual for such achievement is the main aim of creative drama (or improvisation in secondary-school theatre);

(b) the individual's behavior is directed toward a creative product in participational theatre; and

(c) the finished product *per se* is the concern of presentational theatre.

But, because participational theatre incorporates children's creativity, it is also concerned with the ways in which images connect with imagings, in spontaneous creation within a medium, or even discovering that a "problem" exists. Gilchrist's three frames of reference might, more appropriately, be called "discovery," and discovery is imagined conception.

Consciousness has the power of conceiving in imagination—coming forth with a product that has been fused by imagining. The artist works with an imagined conception and externalizes it in action through the chosen medium. Similarly with the child in participational theatre: He or she externalizes an imagined conception in spontaneous dramatic action. In neither case does the imagined conception have to be complete before he or she commences. Many artists have semiformed conceptions until the moment when the artwork is complete, and participating children can work similarly. Active mental structures have their own individual ability to function. This includes an ability to image which plays a valuable role in all creative activity.

Imaging

Images are units with which mental structures work. The term "imagery" is ambiguous. It can refer to both process and product. As product it refers to cognitive figural or spatial constructions. As process it can either be a response to external stimulus (e.g., presentation) or act as a stimulus itself to a mental response. Helen Durio summarizes the modern psychological literature as demonstrating three roles for imagery:

(1) Imagery is a biologically primitive coding and processing system.

(2) Imagery is a developmental stage of mental processing that is seen extensively in children before language skills develop.

(3) Imagery is an adjunctive function used by persons of all ages to facilitate cognitions.[11]

Yet, within the theatre experience, image activity can be described as "known" or "unknown" by consciousness. Some images are "known" in that we can consider them objectively within the waking state. Obversely, there are "unknown" images like those of dreams that only occasionally can be recalled when we are awake. Additionally, there are images that are on the borderline between the "known" and "unknown," and it is these that appear to be at the center of the dynamic for our imagined conceptions. Sometimes called the preconscious or subliminal mind, Galton said the borderline was "the presence-chamber and the ante-chamber" of consciousness,[12] while Coleridge indicated that "ideas and images exist . . . on the vestibule of consciousness."[13]

The mechanisms of these types produce certain differences. "Unknown" images appear to work in an autonomous manner (similarly to those that occur in trance states). Mind is not *overtly* concerned with reinterpreting them into external action, rather being concerned with internal self-experience (or "rest"); whether it is *covertly* so, of course, is open to question. "Known" images appear to be of two main kinds: Those of recall are mainly "reconstructions" rather than "recollections" of past percepts, and those that are imagined are created by the mind through combining other known percepts (e.g., the philosopher's unicorn).

Despite these distinctions, all are active while the student is within the theatre experience. Stekel has indicated that there is a total polyphony of thought.[14] But we can go further because there is a parallel with perception. Although looking at a steeple, I also register things in my peripheral vision although I am not conscious of them most of the time. In all sensory modes, "unknown" percepts are creating "unknown" images all our waking lives (at least), and *all of these* contribute to the evolving structures of the student in the theatre experience.

The Borderline

In the best theatre experience, students' mental constructions work in the borderline state. This occurs with any combination of "known" and "unknown" images. Although most obvious in hypnagogic and hypnopompic states, it can also be detected in hallucinations, eidetic and crystal images, states of synaesthesia, *déjà vu,* and in diagram forms and body schemas.[15] (Thus, for example, many teachers of creative drama use synaesthetic techniques for maximum creativity.)

It can be most clearly observed in participational theatre through what Koestler calls "Knight's-move thinking."[16] The mind of the participating child suddenly combines two images (or groups of images) that are seemingly disparate; often the linking image, associating the two, is not made conscious. Harold Rugg said that borderline activity is relaxed yet magnetic. Resembling the light trance of hypnosis, it is not hypnotically induced or controlled;[17] yet we should note that there is some similarity with the atmosphere of theatre. William James indicated that this state has more affinity to states of feeling than to states of intellect.[18] Thus it seems to those who experience the borderline (including students in theatre) that it provides insight into the depths of truth. It becomes *significant* experience (which is essential for learning).

Kubie indicated that in the borderline we can think of many things at the same time. Yet, if we wish to transfer these into waking states, we can only do so one at a time because the working of waking states may be primarily verbal.[19] There may be some physiological basis for this: Visual imagery appears to be more dependent on the physical similarity of stimuli and spatial context, and is dominated by the right hemisphere of the brain; verbal processing seems to depend more on the ability of the left hemisphere to recall abstractions of past experiences.[20] Thus participational theatre appears most successful when students are acting within the performance rather than, as in some cases, merely talking about the action.

It is in the borderline that the image achieves much of its dynamic work. It is active in much the same way that the body itself is active. The human organism is constantly in a state of motion, and movement produces energy —in the case of theatre, both potential and kinetic. But in a developmental sense, it is the identification/impersonation mechanism that initiates the movement.

The creativity of students occurs in theatre when their mental constructs are working in the borderline state. Images, like all bodily elements, produce energy that allows them to be active. Arising in the borderline, the student's imagined conception is relaxed yet magnetic and thus suddenly fuses disparate elements. These connections are creative in that they are unique and original to that consciousness. What is achieved is discovery. In these terms the student is precisely *not* solving a problem, categorizing in order to achieve a concept or what Bruner calls "concept attainment."[21]

I would agree with Rugg that creation of any type, and specifically that

of the student in theatre, is a flash of insight—an act of knowing that is a
"grasping." This is intuitive identification. This is not to distinguish intuition from knowledge but rather to consider them as *exactly the same thing.*
Thus it includes both Russell's "knowledge by acquaintance" and
"knowledge by description," G. E. Moore's *ipso facto* knowledge, as well as
the existentialist's "felt knowledge." Creation as discovery involves a cognitive grasp of the event but within the intuitive matrix—as a *whole.* The
objective element of the act (the participation) is set within the subjective
matrix (identification/impersonation). The oscillation of mind is between
poles of the "me" and the "not me," where the "not me" is also oscillating
between projection and introjection. This occurs structurally whether the
basis is *who I am* internally (identification) or expressed externally (impersonation). Silberer has shown that images are transformed from the "unknown" to the "known" suddenly, and without conscious control, by the
conflict of two "antagonistic elements": the hypnagogic state and the effort
to think consciously.[22] This is precisely the condition of participational
theatre: the borderline and conscious states overlap, and the elements of
"me" and "not me" are in active oscillation.

Action

Thus we can see that, within participational theatre, the student's mind
acts. It identifies (at its own level of oscillation) with the product of the
fusion of the two elements, which is more than an amalgam of both. The
mental spark takes place as images rise from "the vestibule" into the
"known"—but, normally, they must have been in "the ante chamber" (at
least) to fuse. The created work of art of participational theatre results
from an identificatory process built within its structure. Without it the play
is a failure. In this sense, the creative act of consciousness is a dramatic
action. It is meaning-giving and so provides the context of meaning for the
theatrical work of art.

THE STUDENT AND THE THEATRICAL ENVIRONMENT

Whether the student is a percipient or a participant, his or her mental
structures are not merely subjective. Descartes' *cogito* is always paramount,
of course, but in that structures are created through the activity of relating
inner and outer, they can also be viewed from the point of view of objectivity. In this sense, all mental structures can be seen as socially determined
(e.g., by scientific mechanists, dialectical materialists, behaviorists, and by
many modern sociologists). However, as we shall see, this is open to
question.

The nature of the balance between inner and outer is a shared concern
in the literature, and each writer makes his own case for his particular point
of view. For example, Koestler indicates that, logically, creative activity is
the discovery of hidden similarities while, emotionally, these can be on a
continuum from aggressive, through neutral, to sympathetic and identificatory. The method of discovery, he says, can be through

(1) *a matrix*—the pattern ahead, representing the total possible
movements;

(2) *a code*—the specific rule determining which moves are permitted;

(3) *a strategy*—determined by the environment.[23]

Each of these three methods is determined, to a lesser or greater extent,
by consciousness' acknowledgment of the objective. Frank Barron, however, is very specific about this acknowledgment when he says:

> human nature is an emergent differing in kind from the material and
> from the rest of the organic universe; it is not only the newest thing in
> the universe, *it alone can generate novelty and resist adaptation by an act of
> will.* Before it all novelty arose by chance; with it, novelty can arise by
> intention.[24] (italics are mine.)

The student in the playhouse (like us all in existence) exists primordially
within an internal world. Yet this world depends on what occurs in the
playhouse (the environment) and its relationship to us. The way we handle
this relationship determines our particular "point of view." The student's
existence is made up of a dynamic between the self and the theatrical
world, between subjectivity and objectivity. This occurs through the student's imaginings, which become externalized in actions: physical actions in
participation, mental actions in presentation. That which is of the environment is an object or thing. Yet, as Sartre says, "I am no thing." Genetically,
through Winnicott's "mediate objects" and the primal act of impersonation
at ten months old, the student has recreated the external world of things
within himself or herself. Steadily, through maturation, he or she has developed internal structures that constitute the "felt world." One of the
external things he or she meets is theatre, and this is recreated within the
individual's "felt world."

Yet being human implies a social being. The student's inner world and
what Husserl calls the "everyday world" interlink in such a way that the
social world is made up of the way in which individual world structures
meet. This can take place in the home, at school, or at any time between a
number of people—and it takes place in the playhouse. The context of the
social world consists of aspects of our own worlds expressed as social action.
Genetically considered, the first elements of our structures are directly

derived from the environment. Babies have no choice but to accept the parents they have; the continuous modeling process can provide us with choices only from among the people available to us. Our environment, therefore, has a considerable impact on our innate ability to shape our consciousness in the ways we require. This raises certain fundamental questions: What types of modeling processes affect students' responses to theatre? And which types of theatre produce what kinds of modeling in students?

In terms of modeling, the environment affects the structures (and thus the creativity) of students in relation to the people they meet and the degree of dependence they place on them. This also applies, with acute specificity, to those they meet within a drama.

Sociologically expressed, this can be viewed in (at least) three contexts: *social institutions, material culture,* and *psychological climate.*

It is people who, objectively, most affect the student. In terms of social institutions, it is the family life, social organizational patterns, language and similar elements that affect the creation of mental structures. These elements are not merely important in the personal development of the student but have related significance in *how they are met within the playhouse.* Differences in family life can be decisive. For example, the imitative actions of stimulus and response, characteristic of many white North American homes, presents a different environment to the child's emerging structures from the family life of the Kwakiutl Indian, where, on the more remote reserves, the free and relaxed permissiveness of ancient times can still prevail. Different patterns of child-rearing relate to dominant traits of family life and, therefore, to emergent mental structures.[25] There are variants, too, between those living within longitudinal families and those reared only with parents and siblings. The latter now characterizes Western civilization with the family relating to: a) outer groups of the same family; b) social groups further removed—the school and the peer group. In earlier forms of society such groups had specific organic and religious significance (such as the Amerindian "dancing societies"), but, for Western children, they are liable to be less meaningful. Clearly, identification will vary and, as a result, so will mental structures, according to the social institutions that affect the consciousness.

A significant aspect of social institutions is language. It has a considerable effect on mental structures. The Sapir-Whorf Hypothesis[26] demonstrates (for example) that the type of mental classification expressed by the English language is one thing, while for Amerindians and Innuit it is quite another. Language demonstrates different understandings of the world. But language is different from *any* understanding even though it reflects it.

The language of the society to which the student belongs does not determine his or her innate *apprehension* (feeling, or Gestalt, of the world), but it does influence their *comprehension* of the external world through classifications.

In such ways social institutions affect modeling processes, which bring about mental constructs and, therefore, affect students' responses to theatre. But in each of the above elements we can turn the problem around: What types of social institutions within theatre affect the constructs of students? This is a serious and urgent question and requires attention.

In terms of material culture, the student's consciousness meets with those who are part of a total economic system that belongs to *now*. The ethos within material existence differs in each culture, and in each period, so that each has a different influence on consciousness. The student can only have reflected back to him or her what it is possible for the material culture to reflect. But is this the case in the playhouse? What aesthetic effects are there, for example, on the mind of a child if he is in a New York playhouse in 1977 (where the designer has masses of fabrics, designs, and uses) compared with the student in a small Russian community in 1977 (limited fabrics, colors, largely historical designs, and specifically utilitarian intentions)?

In terms of psychological climate, each society has its own climate as well as varieties within it: between Russia and America; between Moscow and Leningrad, or New York and Los Angeles; or between Watts and other areas of Los Angeles. There is even a different psychological climate within each family group. Each student is affected by the psychological climate of his or her immediate family and by the wider climates within which it exists. This is particularly the case with mores, or the specifically sanctified rules or customs of a living society. But if this is true in the way the child's structures have evolved, how much more true is it of the psychological climates in differing playhouses? What is the structural effect on the child of the psychological climate of the Old Vic as against Theatre Centre, of Story Theatre as against the presentations of the Seattle Junior League, of a small improvisational-participation group as against the splendors of the Moscow Children's Theatre? These, too, are questions that need answering.

The influence of the environment on mental structures, seen in these three sociological contexts, is largely on the understandings the student attempts within the modeling process. Previous individuals have found methods of understanding existence, and these are reflected back to the student. One such reflection is theatre. According to the society in which the student lives, therefore, he or she will have demonstrated, as a model,

several diverse theatrical understandings. It is these with which the identifi-
cational processes must work in order to create the student's world
structures.

But is the environment as all-pervasive as behaviorists and dialectical
materialists would have it? Barron, as we have seen, would think not. He
considers that all depends on Will. Will, the tap root of the Hebraic tradition, has its place in ultimate reality as the will of God, whereby He creates
and governs the world; God's will is good, and so is man's, except where
man sins by willing to go against the will of God. In contrast, the Greeks saw
Reason as the principle of order and regularity, stability and externality, in
both man and the universe; thus occurred the ideas of perfect definability
(e.g., Plato's Forms, the laws of nature and logic) whereby Will acts rightly
only when assenting to Reason. In the Christian synthesis of Augustine,
however, reason and will are identical in God, who is perfect, but never in
man, who is imperfect. In contrast, Hindu and Buddhist would reject Will
for will-lessness and Reason for intuition. Whatever theoretical framework
is used, therefore, apart from the determinist, the environment as such is
not seen as the crucial factor. Pruyser indicates[27] that when the Christian
places his emphasis on God, he does so in terms of St. Paul's sense of the
"me" and the "not me." Inner and outer interpenetrate in play:

> "the private experience may be told as a general human story, and the
> facts of history may be expressed as a personal drama. Things may
> become impersonated and people may be staged as things."
>   This paradox of the me which is also not-me is the essence of
> religion. A Christian statement of it is St. Paul's "I live, yet no longer I
> but Christ liveth in me" . . . is it not a central tenet of Christian
> orthodoxy that grace does not destroy nature but perfects it?[28]

We can see, therefore, the primordial identification/impersonation complex, and the intermediate position of play between inner and outer, as the
genetic origins of all subsequent cultural worlds—arts and science, religion,
politics, and education.[29]

The environment, it can be seen, is set within the matrix of the student's
subjectivity. The "me" has primacy over the "not me." This is significant in
the relationship of children and theatre because it indicates to playwrights
and directors, actors and designers just where their emphases must be
within the dramatic discipline.[30]

CONCLUSION

The student, whether as percipient or participant, co-creates the theatrical artwork. Like the others involved (writer, actor, director, designer) he

is, in this sense, an "artist." The active mental structures of each such theatrical artist, within the context of the environmental feedback we have examined in the previous section, intend the work of art. The inherent subjectivity of the student's mental structures relates to the environment of the playhouse in two ways: a) as input through perception and b) as output of artistic action. Yet, whether as input, output, or feedback, *choice* is the predominant factor. Perception is the basis of, but not the same as, an image.[31]

We have already seen that remembering is based on the remnants of past percepts (it is "reconstruction" rather than "recollection") in such a way that the student's mind is active in relation to images and imagery. It has choice as to which images it will reconstruct and to what degree it will reconstruct them. Choice is always available to the mental structure that is to apprehend, and thus co-create, the work of theatre art. Moreover, the student's action that results is always socially intentional because it is derived from the dramatic qualities (the identification/impersonation complex) of imagination. In similar ways, the student within an audience always has choices as to *what* and *how* he or she apprehends, as well as what significance he or she gives to such apprehension.

The way in which a child's mental structures relate to theatre is determined only by the environment in so far as consciousness permits. In that a child's inner structures are intentional, creating the worlds with which he or she works, they take meanings from (and give meanings to) the environment in their own terms. Yet, in the everyday world, what the child perceives and creates is determined to some extent by the choices available at that time—by the mental "sets" with which he or she is working. Developmental studies of all types show that "sets" are cumulative products of the manifold experiences that the child comprehends. The student's choice is limited by present "sets," except that previous choices may have so altered the cumulative products prior to that specific moment in time that the child may, or may not, be able to break "sets." This indicates the importance of early experience in the arts, including drama and theatre. While it is difficult to break "sets," to splinter the determinism of the past, it is the natural result of previous creative choices.

In this sense, the student is always free. "Making up one's mind" is a human ability. Creating or perceiving theatre is just such a choice.

NOTES

1. See my "Drama and Aesthetics," in *British Journal of Aesthetics* 8, 4, 1968, pp. 373–86.
2. It is Langer's lack of ability to account for this that is the subject of my "On Langer's Dramatic Illusion," in *Journal of Aesthetics & Art Criticism* XXIX, 1, 1970, pp. 11–20.
3. This also accounts for such phenomena as "pop art," where ordinary objects are accorded the status of art objects.
4. See my "A Dramatic Theory of Imagination," in *New Literary History* II, 3, 1971, pp. 445–60; "Imagination and the Dramatic Act: Some Comments on Sartre, Ryle and Furlong," in *Journal of Aesthetics & Art Criticism* XXX, 2, 1971, pp. 163–70; "Education Is Play," in *Childhood Education* 49, 5, 1973, pp. 246–50; "Imagination and Substitution: The Personal Origins of Art," in *Connecticut Review* 9, 2, 1976, pp. 67–73; "Dramatic Action: A Genetic Ontology of the Dramatic Learning in the Very Young Child," in *Journal of the Canadian Association for Young Children*, November 1976, pp. 16–21.
5. D. W. Winnicott, *Playing and Reality* (London, 1974).
6. Alfred Schutz, *The Phenomenology of the Social World* (Evanston, Ill., 1967).
7. Sara Smilansky, *The Effects of Sociodramatic Play Upon Deprived Children* (New York, 1972).
8. J. L. Moreno, "The Creative Theory of Personality," in *New York University Bulletin, Arts and Sciences* LXVI, 4, 1966, pp. 19–24.
9. See my "Theatre and Spontaneity," in *Journal of Aesthetics & Art Criticism* XXXII, 1, 1973, pp. 79–88.
10. M. Gilchrist, *The Psychology of Creativity* (Melbourne, 1972).
11. Helen Durio, "Mental Imagery and Creativity," in *Journal of Creative Behavior* 9, 4, 1976, pp. 231–44. See also my "Creativity and Theatre for Children," in *The Stage in Canada* 7, 2, 1972, pp. 6–15.
12. Francis Galton, *Hereditary Genius* (New York: new edition, 1952).
13. Cited in Harold Rugg, *Imagination* (New York, 1963), pp. 40–41.
14. Wilhelm Stekel, "The Polyphony of Thought," in David Rapaport, *Organization and Pathology of Thought* (New York, 1951), pp. 313–14.
15. Peter McKellar, *Imagination and Thinking* (London, 1957); *Experience and Behaviour* (London, 1968).
16. Arthur Koestler, *The Act of Creation* (London, 1964).
17. Rugg, *Imagination*.
18. William James, *The Varieties of Religious Experience: A Study in Human Nature* (New York).
19. Cited in Rugg, *Imagination*, p. 77.
20. Cited in Durio, "Mental Imagery and Creativity," p. 238.
21. Jerome S. Bruner, J. Goodnow, and G. Auston, *A Study of Thinking* (New York, 1956). For a critique of Bruner on this point, see Richard M. Jones, *Fantasy and Feeling in Education* (New York, 1968), pp. 87–124.
22. Herbert Silberer, "Report on a Method of Eliciting and Observing Certain Symbolic Hallucination-Phenomena," in Rapaport, *Organization and Pathology of Thought*.
23. Koestler, *Act of Creation*.
24. Frank Barron, *Creativity and Personal Freedom* (New Jersey, revised, 1963), p. 302.

25. Sylvia Brody, *Patterns of Mothering* (New York, 1956). See also John W. M. Whiting and I. L. Child, *Child Training and Personality* (New Hampshire, 1953); Robert R. Sears, L. Rau, and R. Alpert, *Identification and Child Rearing* (Stanford, Calif., 1965).

26. For a summary, see my, *Play, Drama and Thought* (London and New York, 3rd rev. ed., 1974), pp. 254–57.

27. Paul Pruyser, *Between Belief and Unbelief* (London, 1976).

28. H. A. Williams, "Hart's Reasons," in *Times Literary Supplement,* March 5, 1976, p. 268.

29. Peter L. Berger and T. Luckman, *The Social Construction of Reality: A Treatise in the Sociology of Knowledge* (New York, 1966).

30. See my "The Discipline of Drama," in *Queen's Quarterly,* 84, 2 Summer 1977, pp. 231–43.

31. S. J. Segal, *Imagery: Current Cognitive Approaches* (New York, 1971). See also my "Imagination and the Dramatic Act."

Grigore Pogonat was born in 1929 in Romania, where he was educated as an actor, director, and teacher. He received his B.A. degree in literature, was graduated from the Institute of Theatre and Film in Bucharest, and received a Diploma in Arts from the Caragiale Institute. In 1974 he was awarded a Certificate for the Teaching of Dramatic Expression by the University of Montreal.

From 1955 to 1957 Mr. Pogonat was a professional actor and the director of the Popular Theatre in Galati, Romania. For the next seven years he was actor and director at the Ploiesti State Theatre and from 1964–1973 was at the Ion Creanga State Theatre in Bucharest. He has taken numerous international tours of his productions for children, including appearances in Albany (ASSITEJ) and New York City in 1972.

Mr. Pogonat has made three films, published articles on theatre, and was the keynote speaker at the Children's Theatre Association of America convention in Los Angeles in 1976. There has been great admiration for his work, hence his contribution to this book is a welcome inclusion. Grigore Pogonat is presently professor in the Theatre Department of the University of Moncton in Canada.

CONSIDERATIONS IN CHILDREN'S THEATRE

3

GRIGORE POGONAT

I would like to specify, right at the beginning, that this essay makes no pretention of solving the many problems in the field of theatre for children. It intends rather to share the thoughts, questions, and concerns of somebody who is dedicated to theatre and who for many years has been particularly involved in children's theatre.

Dear colleagues, let me first emphasize one point that is very important to me. As far as I am concerned, there is only *one theatre* from the aesthetic point of view. All separation between children's and adult's theatre should be used only to differentiate two kinds of audiences. Unfortunately, we often make this division based on aesthetic criteria. Theatre as an art is indivisible, and the dichotomy between theatre for children and theatre for adults is usually to the discredit of children's theatre. Normally, performances for children should present the same qualities of care and aesthetic, of research and ingenuity as those expected from performances presented to adults. All compromises that we are tempted to make in children's theatre weakens the theatre as a whole because children will be the adult audience of tomorrow.

I remember with pleasure Stanislavsky's opinions about theatre for children. Somebody asked him one day, "How shall we act for children?" Stanislavsky answered spontaneously, "Exactly as we do for adults but better." Superb remark, isn't is? But do we always do it?

One day at a cocktail party in Paris I asked a well-known actor what his criteria were in evaluating a play for adults and a play for children. He answered me, without hesitation that he had only one set of criteria to evaluate both kinds of plays. For him, it was very simple. We have good and bad performances on both sides and for the same aesthetic reasons, among which he pointed out as examples, the quality of the play, the artistic and technical solutions found by the director, the atmosphere and the unity of the performance, the sincerity and expressiveness of the actor's work.

Theatre is one, whole and indivisible; that's my opinion. It might be why we often find adults enjoying a good performance for children. An adult may find satisfactions on an aesthetic level in a children's play. Of course he also finds a return to childhood, and we should not forget the interest that one may find in observing children's spontaneous reactions during a show.

I don't want to overemphasize but I do want to underline at the beginning, that, for me, the only difference between theatre for adults and children lies in the nature of the audience. Any other demarcation confuses the issue.

In this article, I shall concern myself with three topics: 1) The child audience and its particularities; 2) acting for child audiences; 3) theatre for children in the era of television.

THE CHILD AUDIENCE AND ITS PARTICULARITIES

Children are a very special audience—I would even say unique. It is a great joy to have an audience of this quality.

First, children come to theatre without prejudice, with an open and innocent mind. We shall acknowledge the fact that children are not much influenced by publicity or by reviews. They usually don't come either for the name of a director or of a star.

A child audience is not yet settled in its taste by its intellectual background or by its education; it has not had time to crystallize its perceptions, as an adult audience has. It is still flexible, malleable, and open. That's why children can accept more easily all kinds of theatre. They don't mind if what they see is called "traditional" theatre, "less traditional" theatre, or "avant-garde" theatre. All they need is to be convinced, to be involved. It is our job to make them react, to touch them, to make them laugh, cry, to amaze them. But we should not forget that children have their own expectations that can be even more disturbing than those of adults. Children cannot make believe they enjoy a play when they are not interested. They are spontaneous in their reactions, wholehearted and sometimes not even polite. If the show doesn't appeal to them, they become restless. They begin to talk and play with each other; the oldest may even leave the theatre. They have perfectly natural reactions to something that doesn't interest them, that bores them, that might not meet their real needs and expectations. It might be because of the play itself, because of the content or because of the expression.

So one important characteristic of a child audience is *spontaneity*. If director and actors are skillful enough to catch the children's attention, the children will easily get involved in the play. When completely involved in the action, sometimes children don't distinguish between acting as a form of expression and reality. For them it is real, all the same. This is especially true for younger audiences.

However, we should not manipulate the spontaneity of children to hide some weaknesses in the play. Unfortunately, there are some directors who for lack of creativity or convenience are tempted to use tricks and "clichés" that are known to work with children. It is always more difficult to produce a really creative work, a work of research. But theatre should be like this, and this includes theatre for children.

I am more and more convinced that, in order to work in the field of children's theatre, one has to love children, to understand them, to respect them and to feel at ease in the children's complex and fascinating world.

As far as I am concerned, a real creation in the field of children's theatre can be done only by artists who have kept a child's soul, together with the intelligence, the formation, the experience, and the culture of an adult.

ACTING FOR CHILD AUDIENCES

And now I would like to talk about actors who act for child audiences. I want to spend a little time on this topic because actors are an extremely important element in theatre in general and, of course, in children's theatre. An actor must translate to the spectators the meaning of the play. Without his soul, without his skills, without his talent, theatre cannot be a full experience, even if the other artisans involved are extraordinarily good.

I want to emphasize particularily good *acting formation*. Actors working for children do not have an easier job than those working for adults. On the contrary! It is a mistake to think that almost any actor can act for children. Very often acting for children is even more difficult than acting for adults.

We often notice that children can easily accept a lack of technical means in a play. Their inventiveness and their imagination make up for it, provided that actors are lively and expressive.

I would like to quote here Peter Brook in an interview he gave to a French journalist. (So please excuse the translation.) "Only one thing cannot miss in theatre; it is 'life.' Theatre does not exist in boredom. Theatre has to be living, otherwise it is unbearable." We could discuss at great length what "living" is in theatre. But with this we could write another book. Anyway, each of us has an idea of what is alive, if only by opposition to what is not, or to boredom.

The life of a play rests on the actors' shoulders. They have the responsibility, the job to translate to the audience the ideas, the meanings, the
feelings, the conflict of the play. They have to reach the spectators. In
order to do that actors must master their own expressiveness. In most cases
natural talent is not enough to meet the artistic work asked of actors. I am
not talking here of special cases, of great talents, of geniuses who, by their
very powerful intuition, can perform superbly even without years of study.
I am talking about normally gifted people who have to nurture their talent
and learn their craft.

Actors, like other artists, must master technical skills, must have developed their expressivness. A good training program provides the basic tools.
If an actor, for example, hasn't trained his voice properly, even if he finds
the inner force to express a feeling, even if he is moved and able to move
the spectators, his untrained voice, husky and tired, may produce a completely unexpected effect. The same thing applies to the body.

Every one of you knows how important it is for an actor to have a good
professional training, in order to develop and master expressiveness. Only
when an actor masters his craft, masters the technical skills of the stage,
only then can he act with pleasure and ease. Theatre for children asks
much of its actors. They must be able to produce without exhaustion. To be
tired prevents an actor from enjoying himself in his work.

And the pleasure of acting is one of the keys to success in theatre for
children. The joy, the pleasure of acting reaches out to the audience. It
warms up the acting situation and the atmosphere in general. Sometimes I
like to think of a play for children as a celebration of expression. The
genuine pleasure of expressing feelings and situations should be natural to
actors, and then the audience will feel it.

If an actor can transmit his joy of acting, he can also transmit his fatigue
and his difficulties of expression. The audience will feel it, to the prejudice
of the play. The only way not to be tired is to be well trained.

I am tempted to emphasize the importance of basic training for actors
because I notice there is a tendency sometimes to be less demanding of
actors in children's theatre. Sometimes theatre for children is considered a
marginal theatre, an easier genre that doesn't require the same skills.

But if what we want is to introduce children to theatre, to familiarize
them with *theatre as an art,* we then have to work at the level required by this
art. I believe that working at this level we also educate them better and
more easily, make them more sensitive, and give them more knowledge.

Let us think for a minute of all the skills an actor needs to express with
his body, what is asked of him in a children's play. At times the actor must
pantomine; he must dance, act with masks (and we know well the importance of the body when the face is covered). At times he symbolizes elements of scenery, elements of nature and natural phenomena; he can be a

tree, waves, fire, tempest, etc. Body expression is important in theatre for children. Therefore, the actor has to be able to communicate with his body a great variety of expressions.

And this takes me to another point: When we work for children, we have to remember that everything must be communicated with precision, clarity, and expressiveness. Precision, clarity, and expressiveness are of extreme importance in theatre for children. I shall underline this: Confused and ambiguous acting, acting without contour or coherence, is not accepted by a child audience. Children must understand without difficulty or effort what is going on on the stage. If they don't understand, if they get confused, their attention and interest in the play will vanish.

In order to catch and keep children's attention, everything has to be expressed carefully. Actors have to take the time to express the things in a complete way.

Do not stop halfway, do not juggle. Of course, each play has its own rhythm, and we have to take into account that the action may require speed. In those cases, we have to find ways of expressing things quickly but not at the expense of quality and comprehension. We also have to take into account the age of the children for whom we perform. Perceptual and intellectual faculties and attention span will vary from a group of younger children to a group of older children. I don't want to develop this point here, but I want to stress the importance of precise, clear, and expressive acting in any performance for children.

I would like to touch briefly on one more point that we must not forget when we talk about the actor's task in children's plays.

In most performances for children, the stage is very close to the audience, if not in the middle of the audience. So the contact of actor with children, the interrelationship of actor with children, is very important. Actors have to be able to make this contact, to relate with the children in a very natural way. No artificiality, no strain, no empty display, and especially *no abuse.* The dialogue between children and actors must always stay in connection with the action. It is part of the play, not something added from the exterior as a device.

So, to draw a conclusion, as much for the quality of theatre for children as for the professional satisfaction of actors themselves and of directors, I stress again the importance of good training for actors performing for child audiences.

THEATRE FOR CHILDREN AND TELEVISION

We all know what impact the advent of television has had on theatre for children. And I agree that the competition is severe. Television networks have, of course, greater technical, financial, and advertising means than we have. We are obliged to face this fact.

I suggest that, facing this situation, we concentrate on the specific values of theatre art. Let us try to strengthen, to give a new impulse, to theatre for children.

First, I think it is important that children learn to distinguish between theatre as an art and TV programs. A child likes to watch television programs. He can also enjoy going to theatre because he finds there something that television doesn't give him: the warmth of a more direct contact with action, the chance to participate more actively and to be closer to the show.

The actor-audience contact has always been the basis of theatre, the basis of its evolution. If this actor-audience relationship is essential to theatre in general, it is even more important in theatre for children because of the nature of the audience, of its inclination to participate. This dialogue between actor and public, this interrelationship, creates a climate that television doesn't offer to children sitting in their living rooms.

Research on what is specific in the actor-audience relationship could help us to *bring forward* what is done in the field of theatre for children and to improve the quality of performances.

Where can we best do this research? I believe it is in laboratory theatres, because I realize that research done in laboratory theatres has given great stimulation to theatre as an art. So I think it would be appropriate to have more laboratory theatres specializing in theatre for children.

A laboratory theatre can be a theatre in the usual meaning of the word but with a special emphasis on research. A group of people, with the same artistic goals, gathers around somebody interested in research who has a good professional preparation and specific experimental goals. To do a good job, a laboratory theatre should have a permanent nucleus of actors who, by working together, will develop their own specific style.

Here are a few subjects that could be explored by a laboratory theatre for child audiences.

1. The development of the actor must be an important part of the research. We should work on the nature of acting; on how to help actors to overcome their psychological, physical, and intellectual problems, aiming at a type of actor more creative, more imaginative, more expressive, and more in control of his technical skills. We should try to go beyond actors' limits and to discover their still unexplored resources.

2. Another area of research could cover the nature of the child audience, its particularities and the actor-audience relationship. In order to carry out research on those subjects, I suggest that the laboratory theatre ask for the collaboration of consultants, such as psychologists, educators, etc. I have already talked about the nature of the child audience and about the importance of the actor-audience relationship. I won't add more, but I believe more serious research on those matters could have a very positive influence in the development of theatre for children.

3. Research could also be done on production and on staging: trying to find new solutions, new forms of performance, new artistic and technical methods. As I said earlier, children accept performances with poor or simple staging. On the other hand, they love technical effects, gadgets, and elaborate mounting. On this we should be more ingenious, more inventive; and good technical effects are not necessarily too expensive.

4. As one final suggestion, research should be done on the themes or the subjects children like best. This should be done by categorizing for different ages, of course.

Concerning this matter, it could be very useful for laboratory theatres to contact young talented writers and try to convince them to write plays for children. I realize that it is not easy to do so.

Another subject for research could be a more intensive study of "fairy tales" because they have been for so long a well-established classical repertoire. La Fontaine, Perrault, Andersen, Selma Lagarlof; the popular tales of every country have provided the plots of many productions enjoyed by children of all times and places. The fairy tale seems to be a natural type of narrative for the child. It is a linear story where the good and the bad are separated, then rewarded or punished according to a very simple logic.

Why do children like this kind of structure? What needs does the fairy tale meet? Can we draw more and more our inspiration from the tale and find more relevance for today's children? Do fairy tales meet, more than anything else, the inner world of children?

Those questions and all the others we have in mind could be explored by some laboratory theatres. I believe in the efficiency of research done in laboratory theatres. I am aware that many other paths may exist, many other possible formulae could be explored in theatre for children. But my concern here is to raise the artistic level. And I think laboratory theatres could have a positive influence on all aspects of children's theatre. Also, inevitably, this could help us to determine more clearly where we stand in regard to television.

I dream of the day when children will come to the theatre because it really meets their needs. They will then learn to love theatre as an art form and thus become a good public for tomorrow.

Brian Way is probably best known for *Development Through Drama,* a textbook on the rationale and use of drama with children. Published in the Sixties, this book has been popular with teachers and students in all English-speaking countries. Brian Way is also credited with introducing the concept of the participatory play to young audiences. He has written a number of scripts for audience participation, including *The Mirrorman* and *Crossroads,* both widely produced. The latter was first presented in 1957 at the Theatre Centre in London.

Mr. Way has been director of the Centre since 1953. In 1973 it boasted seven companies touring plays to primary and secondary schools as well as sponsoring creative-arts workshops. In recent years he has been in demand as a lecturer and workshop leader. Under the auspices of the Educational Arts Association he was introduced to American teachers in a series of drama workshops. In the following essay he defines his approach and describes his methods.

STRETCHING
THE HEART

4

BRIAN WAY

*N*o dogmatic assertion can or should be made about children's theatre, one of the newest and youngest of the theatre arts. The main basis of such work should be both an interest in theatre *and* an interest in children. If either interest is missing or only partial, then there will be a proportionate imbalance. "Interest in" is possibly more important than "detailed knowledge of" in the early stages, as it makes room for experiment within the environment and circumstances confronting oneself and the community one is in or going out to. New specially designed centers tend to be based on established knowledge and practice from a generation ago. Like most "knowledge," this can usurp the innovative potential.

There is a necessity for some kind of definite and positive objective when considering theatre for young audiences—but not a single objective for all time. One discovery throws up another need; changes of circumstance reveal or bar new opportunities. No one group can perceive, let alone fulfill, the manifold potential objectives that exist within the field as a whole. My own yardstick for the last twenty-five years has been the study of "what is appropriate for the youngsters." About the only objective I find quite deplorable is the commercial view that "kids" are suckers for anything. The exploitation of innocent goodwill arising from this attitude usually results in bad theatre, insincere performances, and shoddy workmanship.

Personally, I have never been able to concern myself with the objective of "making theatregoing audiences for tomorrow." That seems to me to be the business of the theatres of tomorrow. If their wares are exciting and interesting enough, then they will have an audience; if not, then they don't deserve an audience, or else they get the audience they deserve. But I see no necessity to convert or brainwash youngsters into a theatregoing habit in order to preserve the privileged activity of actors and theatres. There is more need for theatres to be aware of the "discoveries" of children's theatre.

Nevertheless, I look on part of my responsibility toward children as one that includes introducing them to all of the arts—opera, ballet, painting, sculpture, concerts, as well as plays—and I will do all that I can to find the "appropriate" introduction for each stage of development of the youngsters to each art in turn. My main basis of introduction will be involvement at their own level, for there will never be a more satisfactory way of appreciating the arts than that of practicing them oneself, not as an imitation of the current fashionable adult manifestation of the art but as a means of discovery and joy in that discovery—that is, joy in creative activity within an uncritical framework, devoid of comparison or destructive evaluation. Whether the involvement and the appropriate introductions lead to a lifetime's interest in the arts, either as audience or as participant, seems to me to be outside my terms of reference. I remember being asked by a teenager in the late 1940s, just after a performance in "the open stage," "Can you tell me where I can see more of this kind of theatre?" In England, at that time, I had to reply, "Practically nowhere." I was able to mention one touring theatre.

At this time, the majority of theatre people in England—unlike America and Russia—looked on the "open stage" as the work of cranks—"great fun, dear boy, but you can hardly call it theatre." Neither for that young person nor for theatre as a whole could I look on the work I was doing as "converting" people to the open stage. I had simply discovered that it seemed an appropriate shape for theatre for young people. They seemed to get more from the theatre experience if the actors and audience were in the same room together, rather than being separated from each other by a proscenium arch or an orchestra pit or both. I found that they were also relieved of the necessity for learning and applying the rules of the game of adult theatre "let's pretend." Let us, the actors, pretend you are not there but that our life on the stage is real, and you are peeping at us through a hole in the fourth wall; and let us, the audience, induge in a similar pretense by keeping still and quiet (except for our laughter—when appropriate—and applause). Let us, in fact, accept that the rules include our full participation with the mind, heart, and spirit but not with our voice (except that laughter, of course) and certainly not with our bodies! Certainly no physical participation!

The late Tyrone Guthrie cleared all this up for me when he said words to this effect: "Why cannot we, the players, simply state that we have come to act a play; and why cannot we, the audience, simply state that we have come to see the players act a play? Let us drop the pretense that it is otherwise, and, if the actors are good enough and the material of interest, then the audience will be 'transported.' Maybe they will even forget at moments that this is only 'a play' and will have a deeply involved experience."

Guthrie said this as an introduction to the idea of the open stage, with the actors and audience in the same room, sharing the same physical and psychological environment together. Although it was not so, he might well have been giving a talk on an approach to children's theatre.

However, having said all of this in my concern for a great deal of children's theatre taking place in the open stage, I must make clear that this does not mean that I am opposed to proscenium theatre, even for young people. It remains an incomprehensible factor of Western civilization that the moment one defends a particular way of life one is automatically assumed to be against another! So my personal concern for the open stage as an appropriate area for many age groups of young people for certain experiences has been interpreted as meaning that I am opposed to any use of the proscenium stage. In fact, I am concerned with certain forms of theatre experience for young people that might most appropriately be achieved on the proscenium stage because of its potential for certain kinds of "illusion," including the mixing of straight theatre with other media such as film, slides, or television. Just as these are appropriate experiences for young people in their own creative art forms, so are they in the theatre situation. The answer is again only possible to the honest inquiry: "What is appropriate for the youngster?" Not "What proves my theory or satisfies and fulfills my ambition?"

Just as I am unable to accept a *raison d'être* for work in children's theatre as one of building audiences for tomorrow, so also am I unable to accept the idea of supplying a preferential alternative to film and television viewing. Simply, I do not wish to do so. In my view, both are potentially the most exciting art forms that exist, and factually both have appeals to young people that make it impossible for us to succeed in "weaning them away." Both make the fullest possible use of the close-up of the human face—an experience deeply imbued in every one of us from infancy, from the period of time when the only visual focus of babyhood is the close-up of Mother's face during feeding; even the experience of other people at this time is the experience of the close-up. Further, both film and television include camera angles—particularly the low-shot and the high-shot—that are also part of our youngest experiences; even some of the processes of editing are similar to those of the young child's play in their juxtaposition of events and their economical movement from one scene to another. At an unconscious level, we are all prepared for TV and films so thoroughly that we are at once at home with both media.

This does not mean that we should not be deeply concerned about both the form and content of film and television, but I do suggest that we are wasting our time if we believe that we can actually "take away" people's interest in these media. We have a tremendous task to help them to become "selective" in their viewing habits, but that is a quite different problem. Meanwhile, I not only accept that these are fine art forms both in their own right and as experiences for young people but, as indicated above, wish that it were possible to incorporate them more frequently in children's theatre, both in the open stage and on the proscenium stage.

The reason I cannot do so is the same reason that accounts for limitations in many areas of children's theatre work, particularly professional children's theatre—the reason of finance. Starkly, dollars or pounds—money is almost the ultimate limitation! At times lack of funds is a fine and inspirational challenge; at others, it is no less than a totally destructive force on the creative spirit.

Once upon a time—and not so very long ago—children's theatre was seen as the poor relation of theatre as a whole. (It is still so as far as priorities are concerned!) But now it is viewed, generally, in a quite different light. Actors see it as "a way in to getting an Equity card." Managements smell out the opportunity for new forms of grant aid, and those in charge of education see a new form of potential visual aid, which may be of direct help to problems of teaching. All kinds of vested interests join to give validity to children's theatre. In one sense they are a kind of hope for tomorrow, a possible guarantee of survival; in another, they are forces that press the minds of participants farther and farther away from one of the most important and viable criteria—the young person and his appropriate needs.

In England, the combination of union demands and the limitations of grant aid mean that the majority of professional children's theatres have to make do with a minimum of personnel, usually from four to six, to cover all of the acting, stage management, direct, or peripheral teaching. From four to six people for everything! Of course, there is a great deal that can be done by so few, and indeed it is true to say that for some age groups, particularly the youngest, that number is more than enough. Nevertheless, for the whole span of such work, for its full potential, the number is impossible.

For this reason alone it is good that nonprofessionals, be they students or teachers or simply adults interested in amateur theatre, become involved in children's theatre. There is so much the nonprofessional can do that is beyond the compass and range of most professional groups. This includes every kind of experiment with large-cast plays and many of the possibilities of such experiments as mixing various media. Even the equipment itself is beyond the purchasing capabilities of the majority of English companies, whereas a group that is formed by an education authority or a university (teacher or student groups) may well be able to call on the use of equipment that is part of their own department and therefore will cost nothing. Furthermore, we have to consider the frequency of theatre experience for children and young people. In England, again, that frequency can, for many areas, amount to one single visit a year, simply because the costs of using a professional company prohibit any further visits. If—and it is a big if—there is reason to believe that children will benefit from having more than one experience a year, then additional visits are going to depend on the work of nonprofessionals, who give of their time (limited) and labor (sometimes untrained and inexperienced) without having to count the cost. There are now, in England, many examples of excellent children's theatre teams giving regular performances to children in their own area. The teams are made up of teachers (who have the advantage of knowing children well), and performances are given both in school time and out of school, on Saturdays or during the holidays. Such teams have the advantages of being able to experiment with all kinds of work that are outside the province of professional companies. They are also able to bring regular theatre to their own communities. Their experiments can also include work in parks, in the street, as well as in the more usual theatre environments. They are, by and large, unfettered by economic considerations.

This freedom to experiment with the environment of the theatre experience is an important part of the work as a whole. There is no one answer as to where children's theatre should be performed, any more than there is a single answer to where *adult* theatre should be performed. If, as seems possible, less than 5 percent of the majority of adults have a wish to attend a theatre, then perhaps, as many fringe groups concerned with theatre in pubs or factories would vouch for, theatre should go to where people are rather than waiting for them to come to the place where the actors conventionally are. So it is with children. I recall with delight the experiences of walking around various parks in costume, ringing a bell, singing, dancing, laughing, with other colleagues, all of us playing a kind of Pied Piper, leading the youngsters to where we were going to act our play. This is all a valid part of children's theatre. But if it leads to a performance to thirty souls—who probably do not have to pay—and the economics of the company depend on two hundred people all paying a particular sum, then there is more hope for a company that can manage without the economic factor, and, again, that is more often than not the nonprofessional who is not dependent on box-office returns.

But—so goes the perennial question—can these amateur and untrained actors perform with the necessary expertise for audiences of children? By and large my experience suggests they can, provided they are prepared to accept the need for training for such specialist work, just as professionals must be prepared to accept the same need for training, over and beyond the "acting training" they may have received at drama school.

To act for children obviously requires certain basic accomplishments, and these can only be mastered by some form of practice.

Whether the actors are professional or amateur, much depends on their fundamental attitude. Actors at auditions for Theatre Centre's company often ask, "What shall I do? I know nothing about children." The reply is always "Well, do what you would do for the National Theatre auditions or the Royal Shakespeare Company; that will at least give us some idea of your quality as an actor."

One hopes that the day has long since gone when actors felt that anything was good enough for "kids." There is a realization now of the need for an intense basic absorption and concentration leading to a depth of sincerity and truth that alone bring meaningful experience to young people. They see also, whether professional or amateur in status, that there is need for flexibility, particularly if any form of audience participation is involved, and that such flexibility is linked with training and practice in improvisation as an art form in its own right. There is also the realization of the need for a free and flexible body and voice, for great teamwork, based on the most stringent forms of sensitivity, and a seriousness of approach that would grace a renaissance of all forms of theatre let alone that specially arranged for children. Let nobody pretend, however, that these necessary qualities suggest the need for another two-, three- or even five-year course. A dedicated and unselfish actor can master many of the needs during a fully determined and fruitful rehearsal period. The mainstay is that of "attitude."

In my experience, both amateur and professional can master the basic necessities, provided their "heart" is in the right place. A big proviso!

So it is with characterization. There is a tendency, particularly in plays for younger children, to think that there is a oneness of characterization, a kind of stereotype that is adequate for "kiddies"! Quite recently I worked with a superb actor who was amazed to hear that children's-theatre kings can be as different from each other as Claudius is from Lear and either of them from Richard III. But, naturally, the factor of characterization is a realm that belongs as much to the playwright as to the actor.

To a large extent the author is dependent on the actor, especially in short plays (forty to forty-five minutes) when there simply isn't time to develop all characters in depth, and there is dependence on the actor to take some two-dimensional cardboard characters and breathe new life into them, often as much to the surprise and delight of the author as to anyone else. This largely intuitive process of creativity by the actor is often not only one of the main cores of children's-theatre work but also can be of great interest and benefit to the actor as well, providing him with imaginative opportunities that he will not always experience in other forms of theatre.

The same kind of acting opportunity also exists in plays that are largely improvised, particularly by groups concerned with such local provision as "Saturday Morning Theatre," with a new play every Saturday, even if it be for an audience of only a dozen or twenty. Theatre Centre, in London, started such a process of Saturday-morning plays over ten years ago. Since then several hundred different plays have been performed, most of them once only, the majority arising from discussion among the participants as to theme and story, and all of them dependent on bold, intuitive characterization by the actors. But it is pertinent to note that the actors are involved in regular improvisation as a part of training and preparation. They have moved beyond the stage of vague ad-libbing.

Improvisation is of primary importance in any form of children's theatre that makes use of audience participation, whether structured, perhaps even rehearsed, whether planned only in rough outline or even if entirely spontaneous and possibly unexpected. Whatever the form of the participation, the actor is invariably involved in having to depart from text, perhaps only for one sentence, perhaps for minutes at a time. Perhaps he will be involved in cutting a whole scene or a whole speech, and he is as likely to have to add a new scene or a new speech. Whatever the occasion, the involvement will include improvisation, wholly in character and with a heightened degree of sensitivity with the other actors concerned in the same moment of the play. It is perhaps true to say that the hallmark of this improvisation at its best is when no one has any realization that there have been any insertions or cuts in the play.

Many actors become so delighted with these experiences of improvisation that they are led to feeling there is no need for a playwright at all. I do not personally share this view, though I acknowledge the point for certain kinds of children's theatre (e.g., the Saturday-morning plays described above), and I can see the necessity in approaches to certain forms of educational theatre where skilled actor-teachers are building some kind of dramatic experience with small groups of children in an in-depth situation over a number of weeks. I can see also the point of a group thought on a basic idea, just as there is invariably value in a group thought about a production problem. Ultimately, however, I feel that the writer's pen is indispensable to most children's theatre.

For some people, the problem is often one of not being interested in the taxing discipline of creating from a text. With others, there is often a sincere political motive concerned with employment of out-of-work actors in some form of group theatre, without leadership of any kind, either from a producer or a writer. Sadly such people forget that writers and producers are also artists and often equally without employment. Sir Tyrone Guthrie used to say he never acted more than was needed to understand the problems of the actor. Are we to lose such great producers to satisfy a political ideology that should be capable of embracing art in its fullness?

But if the writer is concerned with audiences of young children—say, up to the age of about eleven years—then he, like the actors, must be ready to be confronted with audience participation.

Many children's-theatre companies decry the idea of audience participation, stating objections that range from its not being necessary to its not working and therefore not worth considering. Indeed some go so far as to say that people like myself have made some kind of shibboleth out of the idea of participation, which is, in their view, now rather old-fashioned and dated.

It is a little saddening that groups that often debunk audience participation as wholly impractical often ignore the basic and clearly stated needs of the play—e.g., maximum size of audience and size and shape of playing area. One such group performed one of my own plays to over seven hundred children of assorted ages from five to sixteen on a proscenium stage. They were very angry about the participation not working. The play, in fact, was written for a maximum of two hundred nine to eleven-year-olds, sitting around a fourteen-foot circle.

Often the problem also arises from the wrong attitude to the participation, which only works when it is fully sincere and from within character; the actor cannot suddenly become "a teacher."

With all of these interesting points of view, I have to return to my "ultimate criteria—the child itself" (who incidentally does not change fundamentally, as do fashions of theatre!), and I remind myself that neither I nor any other adult *invented* audience participation; we observed it *as fact*. The situation was perfectly clear for the keen observer. If the acting of a group has the qualities spoken of above, then the young child becomes involved, emotionally, intellectually, and spiritually, but, because he does not know the rules of theatre about being still and quiet, his involvement goes a stage further and he wants to help, genuinely to help. This help takes the form of vocal and physical participation. My own first observation of this phenomenon was in theatre of the wrong shape, with the wrong play to the wrong age group—two thousand children from five to fourteen watching a Shakespeare play on a proscenium stage. The situation was, of course, chaotic, with most of the children talking or wandering about the auditorium and many throwing missiles at the actors on the stage. Nevertheless, when I sat with the audience, a few quiet fascinating factors were observable:

(1) The least disturbance came from the front six or seven rows of the audience, those close enough to see the faces of the actors in full detail.

(2) For these same rows, there were moments of simplicity in the play that wholly arrested their attention.

(3) For these same rows, many of the things they were calling out to the actors were based on a genuine and sincere desire to help the people they liked and to thwart the plans of their enemies.

These observations led to my first experiments in children's theatre, which arose directly from the above experiences:

(1) Making sure that all members of the audience could see the actors' faces. This meant moving into the same room as the audience and also confining the numbers in the audience.

(2) Seeking material that was more appropriate to the youngsters—and this also meant narrowing down the age span of each audience.

(3) Preparing the actors for the fact that participation—in the sense of helping—might arise and arranging for us to respond to rather than reject it if it did so.

Within a matter of weeks one had discovered a whole new world of theatre, neither better nor worse than one's traditional experience of adult theatre—simply different, different in almost all of its fundamentals.

The major difference—the one entirely different from experience of adult theatre—was audience participation.

From these earliest experiences came the need for continuous research into two main factors: form and content and to a certain extent direct and intended experiments with audience participation governed both of these factors. The basis of our research was to avoid all temptations to accept "success"—i.e., the immediate thing being tried actually seen to work over and over again—as a means of reaching out toward some kind of formulae. It simply released us to try something else we had not tried before. As an example of this I would quote the number of different openings we experimented with: quiet openings, loud ones, sudden, slow, starting out of the hall or in the hall, seating the children ourselves or letting someone else seat them, with music, without music, with action or with words, with sudden group work or with a single individual, before the assembly of the audience or after that assembly, sadly, happily, gaily, dramatically, and so on. I am still constantly asked, "What is the *ideal* way of opening a play for children?" I can only reply that I do not know of one ideal way. It depends on the content, on the number of children, on the age range of the audience, on the experience of the actors, and on the intention of the author. I still do not believe there is a single ideal type of opening that is fail-safe.

FORM

In terms of form we began at once to discover that the open stage did not mean one single alternative to the proscenium stage. Once out in the open, the actual shapes available were legion—avenue arena, with or without the use of the stage at one end of the room; the "half-round"; the audience on three sides; the complete circle or the square, with the audience surrounding the acting area; the rectangle; the triangle; the oval. And even for certain kinds of play—for example, the family play at Christmas time—back to the proscenium stage but with full use of gangways and the audience area wherever possible.

In the open stage we discovered that lack of scenery—for which we substituted a very simple use of rostrum blocks—meant that form was affecting content, for with no visual and materialistic distraction, it was clear that the quality of absorbed listening increased, enabling us to deepen the thinking area of the play. At the same time we discovered that, having abandoned the illusionary potential of the proscenium stage, it was necessary to have such things as sound equipment and dimmer boards (if lighting were used) in full view of the audience. This at once got rid of the need for the audiences wondering about "where does the music come from and who is making it?" A single glance and their curiosity was satisfied—and their fullest attention returned to the play. We quickly discovered that for certain kinds of play and with younger age groups, lighting was wholly unnecessary and indeed rather confusing and meaningless; so, where appropriate, we dropped it. (This did not mean we raced into making a new rule stating that lighting is not necessary!)

We discovered that the apparent need for gawdy and brilliant colors in costumes was not always true, that for some plays the simplest of dressing-up—yes, even within full view of the audience—was much more appropriate.

We learned entirely new attitudes to "properties" and that in certain plays some properties were necessary while others could be mimed *within the same scene*. For example, we discovered that in *Oliver Twist* all properties that directly affected Oliver were necessary and everything else quite inessential. In Fagin's den it was necessary to have the wipes (the handerkerchief) but at the same time all the cooking of food could be mimed.

We also discovered a lot about such details as actual seating of the youngsters. Those up to the age of eleven were most comfortable on the floor, twelves and thirteens were happy on the floor if they had some kind of mat to sit on, and after that they preferred to be on benches or chairs. Eventually we even discovered that it was wisest to keep the youngest children (the five-year-olds) in a group together rather than spread around the front row, where they lacked security of being with their peers and often felt lost and out of place. In most theatres it is a natural tendency to put the youngest into the front row because they are the smallest. In fact, this is not always appropriate from the youngsters' point of view.

In our research into form, linked again with content, we were also very concerned about a) numbers in the audience and b) actual age groupings. We started with a maximum-sized audience of three hundred and fifty and quickly reduced this to three hundred, thence to two hundred and fifty and finally to two hundred. Each reduction had two effects: 1) It improved all aspects of performance; 2) it destroyed our budget more and more. Indeed, but for grants of various kinds we should not have been able to continue the work at all, at any rate not without prostituting its fundamentals, it real values for each audience. I believe that this is where both private patronage and public money are well spent in children's theatre. It helps to preserve the quality of work by removing box-office pressures. Meanwhile, it is possible that children's theatre is the only form of theatre that states a *maximum* rather than a minimum audience!

Concern for form led to many consideratons regarding the most suitable place for performing to children. Without making any hard-and-fast rule we came more and more to the conclusion that the school was the most appropriate place. Usually it contained a hall of some kind, and it was familiar as an environment to the children. It brought theatre into their own community, like libraries and swimming pools and pubs and shopping centers, and therefore helped to lose the idea that going to the theatre involved a long journey with a packet of sandwiches! And we quickly discovered the value of visiting each school separately rather than having several schools visit another school central to them all. The latter arrangement might help with numbers, but it destroyed the essential homogeneous quality of the audience. This led us into yet new experiences when we found ourselves in remote village schools with perhaps thirty children with an age range from five to fourteen! These circumstances led to even newer discoveries regarding form and content, let alone the potential for audience participation.

CONTENT

The background to this research in England is fundamentally that of the organization of schools. These were (and largely still are): infant schools, age group five to seven; junior schools, age group eight to eleven; secondary schools, age group over eleven, some to as high as eighteen or nineteen.

In earlier times the secondary modern and the grammar schools were quite distinct. In recent times some areas have added a middle school, which absorbs the upper junior and the lower junior.

Early children's-theatre experiments tended to divide age groups quite naturally, based on the school organization, providing one play for the primary age group (i.e., a mixture of the infant and junior, who tended to be housed in the same building under the same head teacher) and the secondary. This meant in the earliest days one performance for three hundred fifty five to eleven-year-olds and another for three hundred fifty eleven to fourteen (fifteens). Where the attitude of schools and education officials was concerned—and the whole idea of the work was very new to them all—it seemed necessary not to experiment with both form and content at the same time. The idea of being in the open stage was quite enough for them to absorb and assimilate, without presenting them with problems of unfamiliar content. So our tendency was to adapt well-known stories that would certainly be familiar to the teachers, if not necessarily so to the young people.

Thus, for juniors, we were concerned with adaptations of books or stories such as *Pinocchio* or stories by Grimm and Andersen. For secondary schools we adapted *Oliver Twist,* Eliot's *Silas Marner,* Buchan's *Midwinter,* and an unknown and obscure book, *Grinling Gibbons and the Plague of London.*

These adaptations had many advantages. They did precisely what we had hoped with teachers and officials—captured their interest—and the teachers were increasingly intrigued by the form and the inclusion of audience participation, which they could understand would not be possible with the same quality or depth if the performance had taken place on the average school stage. But apart from this, we were working with material that had been written by skilled authors, so we were both consciously and unconsciously learning something of the craft of story writing and discovering a great deal about the ways of handling such material for different age groups.

However, it is important to note that material was never chosen simply because it was part of school curriculum study in the hope of winning the support of the authorities. Even when we ventured into the field of Shakespeare, we still never made any kind of reference to school studies. We refused, and still do, ever to use the potential of theatre merely as an audiovisual aid to work already being studied in school. We saw theatre then—and still do now—as an extension of the horizons experience, not a repetition of experience.

Further, because of audience participation, we were deeply involved in the study of the balance in education of intellect and intuition and could see the place of the arts in the development of intuitive experience. This was so even in the language used in the dialogue in the plays. Many times teachers would tell us that such and such an age group of children would not have met and therefore would not understand such and such a word. Indeed, they might not do so as an isolated word, but within context they did, even if there were only intuitive understanding rather than intellectual comprehension. Ultimately this went for story content and the relationship of characters. Many people have been astonished at the range of experience possible for youngsters of all ages through the medium of a play, but it is not necessarily the same experience for all the children at the same time. As one head teacher put it when I asked him if his children had "understood" a most stretching play for nine- to eleven-year-olds, "If you are asking me the degree of intellectual comprehension, then I would say that only ten percent had one hundred percent understanding, and probably twenty percent had no more than ten percent understanding, the remainder varying in between those extremes. However, if you are asking me 'Have they had an intuitive experience?' then I believe one hundred percent had one hundred percent." Another head teacher, in answer to the same question, replied, "When I play my children a piece of music or show them a picture, there is only one question I do not ask: 'Do they understand it?' I believe," she added, "the same view is important with poetry and plays."

We were soon able to see that a play presented to the full age range of five to eleven was likely to provide rather feeble challenges for the top two years. So we split the audience and provided a separate play for the older group, at the same time reducing the maximum audience. Before long we had made another split in the age range by supplying an entirely different play for the infants and again cutting the audience size to two hundred. With the secondary age groups we were eventually discovering the need to have one play for the lower half of the school and another for the upper, again with corresponding reductions in the size of audience.

For one period of time we had five different plays for five different age groups, each of which was receiving a very full and rich theatre experience when seeing the play for the appropriate age range.

This did not mean that we did not continue with experiments with plays for the larger age spans for different kinds of theatre experiences, particularly in terms of family entertainment or for village schools where there were very few children spanning the whole age spectrun.

The principles underlying the choice of material, however, remained. I personally cannot bring myself to use the power of theatre for vested interests of any kind, be they political, religious, or merely academic. This does not mean I do not see theatre as an instrument for sharing social values; it means that I believe theatre is for increasing the span of the heart, not for bending the mind.

AUDIENCE PARTICIPATION

Throughout what I have written so far there are many indications of the prior importance I personally feel for the place of audience participation in children's theatre. The subject is so vast that it really needs a book of its own to begin to do justice to it, for all aspects of children's-theatre endeavor it is perhaps the one that leads to the most misunderstanding, particularly in its actual practice.*

There are, however, several points I feel it is important to emphasize regarding audience participation:

(1) All plays must obviously be concerned with intellectual, emotional, and spiritual participation. The difference, particularly for young children in children's-theatre work, is that they do not know the rules regarding adult theatre, which generally does not look for nor encourage vocal and physical participation.

(2) The amount and degree of physical and vocal participation depends on the objective of the company concerned. For example, when Theatre Centre became deeply involved with the use of participation as a means of helping teachers to see an approach to creative dramatics within the general educational day, it increased and developed the amount of participation in the plays that were presented in the schools.

(3) Genuine participation has little or nothing to do with the old musical hall or pantomime tradition of "making a noise big enough to bring down the roof." Indeed, the reverse may well be axiomatic—that loud and noisy participation usually moves toward hysteria and insincerity and is therefore meaningless. This means that it is very important for actors to gauge the quality of participation by the absorption of response from the audience, not by the volume of response. Particular control is necessary in moments concerning humor, as most actors have a natural instinct to "milk" audience response in such situations.

(4) The actor must always remain totally absorbed in character throughout moments of audience participation, otherwise the resulting insincerity betrays the youngsters' belief in the situation.

(5) Practice and experience within all aspects of improvisation seem to be the finest form of preparation for actors who are to be involved in this kind of theatre.

---

* I am at present writing such a book. It will be published by the Educational Arts Association, Reston International Conference Center, Suite 227, 11800 Sunrise Valley Drive, Reston, Virginia 22091. At least twenty of the plays to which the book refers will also be published.

(6) While it is possible for audience participation to take place in quite large theatres and in performances on proscenium stages, it is always more limited in scope compared to work in the open stage with smaller audiences.

(7) Authors who write for audience participation need to state clearly the intended form of staging, the age group for which the play is most suited, and the maximum audience size. Where these are so stated, performers should expect to adhere to the suggestions in order to achieve the most meaningful experience for the youngsters.

(8) Generally speaking, there are three main types of audience participation: a) the directed; b) the stimulated; c) the spontaneous. Those concerned with drama in education will be interested in this precise parallel with the development of such work.

DIRECTED PARTICIPATION

As its name implies, this form of participation is concerned with direct "instructions" from the actor to the audience. For example, a character says, "Everybody close his eyes and . . ." The actor is stating exactly what is necessary for that moment in the play, because it is an integrated part of the play. He needs total and complete faith that there will be a positive response and needs to accept the response as it comes, without trying to increase it and without making any value-judgment remarks such as "That's wonderful" or "That's the best I've ever seen." In order to make quite clear the moment of starting, the use of the word "now" is often important, and for the moment of completion the use of the word "there" helps in the same way. But the latter is not always necessary, as completion can be seen or felt by the audience in so many other ways that are instrinsic to the dramatic situation.

Directed participation has an affinity with the kind of direct audience address that can be used in soliloquies, but a soliloquy can equally be reflective and to this extent be more indirectly addressed to the audience. So with participation, which can move from the directed to the stimulated.

STIMULATED PARTICIPATION

From what a character says, the indication is made to the audience that there is need of help from them. For example, a character marooned in a calm sea might say, "If only there was a wind I'd soon find my way to land" and probably the audience will at once supply the sound of the wind that helps him. On the other hand, the character's reflection about his predicament may lead to some suggestions of a practical solution from the audience. For example, a character confronted with a problem regarding a journey of some kind might reflectively say, "I wonder what would be the best way of getting there." Many different suggestions may be made, and the situation may be such that the actor can seize on any one of them and use it. On the other hand, the scripted situation may require one of only two alternatives, either of which is certain to come from the audience, and the character then moves forward accordingly, perhaps now changing to *directed* participation in order to enlist the audience's further help. One particular difficulty arises in this kind of participation—namely, that of rejecting, without offense or hurt, suggestions that are not appropriate to the characters intention. But if there is only one intention, particularly if it is one not likely to be thought of by the audience, then it is more sensible and fairer not to solicit their help. Participatation is a thing of feeling and intuition, not a comprehension test!

The balance and interplay of directed and stimulated participation is an intricate and delicate one. Once mastered by actors, it can become a most exciting and exacting form of theatre that depends on the maximum of sensitivity and flexibility. From within such a play the actor feels the total involvement of the audience, even to the extent of feeling that the play cannot progress without their participation. And, of course, it is possible for authors skillfully to write into a play a situation where literally the story cannot progress without the help of the audience. In a play called *The Decision* this was true of a response that led to a vote of two alternative endings to the play, and the vote was often very close indeed, necessitating a genuine recount. The actors had rehearsed two quite different endings— both involving participation—so that the vote could be absolutely honest and not involve any need to try to persuade the vote in a particular direction.

Directed and stimulated participation can both be written into a play, to whatever degree is necessary for the action of the story (not just a gimmick or fashionable trick), and, in rehearsal, the actors can be thoroughly pre- pared for such aspects of participation, despite the fact that there will be essential differences at every performance. However, no matter how much preparation of this kind is considered, there will more than likely, particu- larly with young children, be additional moments of quite spontaneous and unexpected participation, which the actors need always to be ready for and to make swift, intuitive decisions about.

SPONTANEOUS PARTICIPATION

We must have all experienced the moment in a movie when the villain is creeping up behind the hero and an urgent voice calls, "Look out—behind you." According to our degree of sophistication we laugh both at the story and at the moment of actual happening. Nevertheless, this is participation at its simplest and most naïve—and often at its most honest. Since the birth of movies it has happened with youngsters—and it always will when they are young and innocent enough for genuine spontaneous offers of help to take precedence over calculated intellectual assessment of the possible reaction to the offer. (The circle of conversion of generosity of spirit to calculated cynicism appears both inevitable and unbreakable. Incidentally, it is one of the reasons why I do my best to keep parents away from participation plays. They invariably look on the sincere response of children as "cute" and then create bewilderment for the participants by a laughter that one would find cruel except for the realization that it arises from a pathetic insensitivity, unawareness and ignorance.)

Let us consider a possible situation that can so easily arise in a children's-theatre play that includes, welcomes, accepts, and encourages participation by the audience. At one moment, shall we way, those in opposition to the hero set up circumstances to trap him. We hear these circumstances quite clearly; we know both intention and result. If we are very young, if we are witnessing actors whose sincerity is such that they have made the situation real for us, if we have reached the point of suspending all disbelief, then the next time our hero arrives before us we are going to warn him of the dangers ahead and, if necessary, we are going to advise him of a course of action that will avoid the danger. That we do so is the most natural thing in the world; it does not even occur to us that the hero is going to win anyway, that the problems he is confronted with are all there for our fun and enjoyment as part of the play. It would not even matter to us if at such a moment somebody whispered to us that if our advice is accepted we could have half an hour's less entertainment than if we kept our peace and said nothing. We might be satisfied with our hero listening carefully to us, thanking us and promising to be on his guard (and no actor will find a greater challenge to his sincerity of playing than in such a momemt). We might feel reassured to be told that he or she has a counterplot that will foil the enemy, but one way or another our anxiety and genuine interest remains until a satsifactory resolution comes up.

This, at its simplest, is spontaneous participation, often the most challenging of all, if only because of its unexpectedness. Skilled and experienced actors will intuitively find a way of accepting and using such situations. There are hundreds of possible situations that might arise, and each time there will be several different ways of facing up to the situation. More often than not the circumstances of playing will govern the possibilities of choice. For example, Theatre Centre companies work with scripted plays and strongly controlled school time tables. On many occasions the actors have been tempted to follow up a moment of spontaneous participation, which, had they done so, could well have added ten to fifteen minutes to the play, and kept a whole school waiting for lunch, which is scheduled for immediately after the play ends at an agreed minute on the clock. Sometimes the moment of spontaneous participation might well bring rich experience to a small number of participants but wholly exclude another one hundred children in the audience who are not involved in the same way. On the other hand, in the very informal and improvised type of Saturday-morning children's theatre mentioned above, the type of spontaneous participation might lead to completely changing the whole play, but there are probably only fifty children involved in a very free and flexible framework and physical environment.

The readiness of the actor is paramount for spontaneous participation; and, again, training and practice improvisation will always help response to come deeply from within character and situation, rather than being "thrown."

(9) For young children (say up to about nine years of age) participation is best done with the whole audience at one and the same time, sitting where they are. This can include, of course, different parallel activities for two, three, or even four sections of the audience, though this latter is inadvisable, except in-the-round and with an audience limited to about two hundred.

(10) From nine years old to about twelve, some of the audience can begin to participate by joining the actors for such situation as "journeys." Yes, there may be some disappointment for those not selected, but this can be minimized by the sensitivity of the cast in their selection. They need to practice and develop a manner of approach that allows for wholly *arbitrary* selection so that no one feels excluded on such grounds as not being good-looking or clever or attentive or whatever. Indeed the so-called disappointment is considerably less than is often suggested, partly because at this age the youngsters are approaching an awareness of "conscious theatre" and therefore perceive the limitations imposed by the particular needs of the play. In circumstances involving this kind of group participation, with an audience watching the participants, considerable thought must be given by the actors to finding every means of preserving the sincerity of the young people so that there is no encouragement to "show off" or "be clever or cute"—simply, like the actors, to be deeply involved.

(11) From twelve upward there can be involvement in fully conscious theatre; there can be actual rehearsal of participation of all or just a section of the audience. Indeed, working with genuinely interested volunteers can be of paramount importance because of the possibility of self-conscious embarrassment among those who have no particular wish to participate. But rehearsal should be swiftly intuitive and emotionally exhilarating and exciting, not intellectually and academically dull and exacting. The discipline of theatre creation can be seen as an exciting adventure rather than a boring chore. At Theatre Centre a second act of fifty minutes was often included as a crowd scene with from forty to all two hundred of the audi-

ence involved. Only twenty-five minutes were spent rehearsing a scene that lasted twenty-five minutes when performed. The six actors had, of course, already thoroughly rehearsed their major roles, and all would be involved in some way or another helping the rehearsal of the participants. To see the final scene of *Hamlet* rehearsed and played within the span of fifty minutes—and played with an authority, dignity, sensitivity, and excitement that is quite breathtaking, in an entirely bare school hall or gymnasium in broad daylight during school hours—can be something of an "awakening" experience of theatre.

That surely is one of the major points of children's theatre—to awaken the mind and imagination of participants, actors and audience alike.

No dogmatic statements can or should be made about children's theatre. May it always remain youthful, vital, experimental, and intuitive.

PART II

Material for Children's Theatre

The late **Sara Spencer** was a graduate of Vassar College and an early exponent of theatre for children. She was best known as editor and publisher of the Anchorage Press (formerly the Children's Theatre Press), a publishing house she founded in 1935 for the purpose of making available to producers better material than was currently on the market. She began with four titles. By 1976 her list had grown to include 113 plays and nine textbooks. Singleness of purpose and insistence on high quality have earned the Anchorage Press the reputation of being the foremost publisher of plays for young audiences.

Sara Spencer's contribution to the field is by no means confined to publishing, however. She was one of the founders of the Children's Theatre Association of America and its director from 1953 to 1955. She was instrumental in forming the Children's Theatre Foundation and in helping to establish the United States Center for ASSITEJ, the International Association of Theatre for Children and Youth.

She received numerous honors and citations. Among them are an award from the Southeastern Theatre Conference, the Clarke College Thanksgiving Award (1966), and the Jennie Heiden Award from ATA in 1976. There has probably been no better informed person in the United States on the subject of scripts and trends in production. In the following essay Sara Spencer shared her knowledge in a discussion of children's plays, past and present.

A WORD FOR
THE PLAYWRIGHT

5

SARA SPENCER

*I*t was an innocent time. In England a man named Barrie had written a play about a little boy who didn't want to grow up. In Belgium a man named Maeterlinck wrote a play about two children who traveled many paths in search of happiness. In America a Broadway producer named Winthrop Ames gave elaborate productions of *Little Lord Fauntleroy* and *Snow White and the Seven Dwarfs*. In Russia a young woman named Natalia Sats was appointed by the new Soviet regime to establish an extensive system of children's theatres across that broad country. In France a distinguished producer named Chancerel resigned from the adult theatre to form a children's-theatre company in Paris called Le Théatre de l'Oncle Sebastien and dreamed of organizing an international children's theatre assocation.

It was before the days of instant communication or jet travel, and all of these efforts were isolated, tentative soundings into unknown depths that could have washed them out to sea. It is a tribute to these early experimenters that they kept their bearings and stayed afloat, even dipping into deeper waters and eventually embarking on a brave new adventure that has proved to be one of the exciting developments of twentieth-century theatre.

It was 1968 before the formation of the International Children's Theatre Association, known as ASSITEJ, made it possible for children's-theatre producers to come together from many directions—and when they did, the great cry that drew all into a united body was the need for reper-

67

toire. "What do you do in Anchorage?" they said. "I look for plays." "Oh, so do we! Where do you find them? Have you got any today plays?" "Yes, we have a few, but they are not very good." "Oh, neither are ours. How can we get them written?"

The times were not so innocent any more. In England they were giving plays like *The Tingalary Bird*. In Italy they were giving *My Black Brother*. In America we were giving *Reynard the Fox* and *The Ice Wolf*. In Holland children were sent to see *The Crowned Boot* and in Czechoslovakia to *Volpone*.

In Belgium a symposium was held on the relative merits of the fairy tale versus this bolder material. The fairy tales lost the argument—but the fact remained that the best plays given in every country were still the fairy tales.

Perhaps this will always be so. The fairy tales are classics. Their stories are woven of the stuff that enchants children, and each generation has found new meanings in them. They have provided our playwrights with theme, plot, character, dialogue, and spectacle. No children's playwright has been able to match them for sheer ecstasy. No producer has found the challenge and the opportunity for theatrical magic in any other type of play. We salute the fairy tales. Long may they reign!

But no one would wish to be confined to them, and the young producers, in a rebellious swing of the pendulum, evolved the unscripted play. In America this took the form of improvisations, the Living Stage, games theatre. In England it became the Theatre in Education movement. In Germany it gave rise to the political cabaret theatre, all of them dealing with the realistic problems of children in contemporary society and all of them developed by the acting company and by audience responses, without benefit of playwright.

No one was rash enough to suggest that the playwright should go away. Even the audience-participation theatre that originated in England required a playwright to give shape to situations for the audience to participate in. Even the Paper Bag Players, a unique company in America that drew its material from unpretentious workaday happenings, worked from a written script. The playwright took advantage of the situation, learning and incorporating into his scripts new dialogue patterns, new character interplay, venturing into unconventional subject matter, simplifying staging techniques. His plays, inspired by personal philosophic convictions, were often derived from other sources. Those that were original devised plots and situations recognizable to the average child and created characters who commented on matters within a child's knowledge and understanding. From England came a play called *The Thwarting of Baron Bolligrew,* about an unassuming knight thrust unwittingly into a position where he was obliged to defy the threat of big government. From the United

States came a play called *Step on a Crack,* about a tomboy girl whose claims on her father had to be shared with a new stepmother. From France came a play called *The Upside-Down Way,* about a little girl who rebelled against the mold she was brought up to conform to. Also from France came a play called *The Frog Palace and the Bulldozers,* about a farm family defending their bit of country against the encroachments of commercialism. Plays of this kind enlarged the experience of children, expanded their knowledge, and lent the repertoire interest and diversity.

By the 1970s there were about a hundred plays available in the English language that could truthfully be classified as literature, some of them translations from other tongues. This was the result of seventy years' diligent searching, persistent writing, sometimes painful experimentation, and none of them was a great play. But they had come a long way from the dewy days of *Peter Pan*—and even the adult theatre had to wait two thousand years for a Shakespeare.

It is no time to relax. Oh, the plays that need to be written! Plays with characters so real they would touch our souls with love, with understanding, with compassion. Plays with plots so inevitable they could turn out no other way, whether for good or ill. Plays with language so poignantly used that the result would be pure poesy. Plays with ideas so brave, so compelling, they could light the way for a new generation. Plays so pregnant with extended meanings they would give rise to divine music. Plays so rich with imagery they would call for new breakthroughs in designing, costuming, lighting. Plays that would establish the children's theatre as an art form.

To create such plays the authors do not write just for children, though they address their material to children. They do not write just for money, though they are entitled to a fair compensation for their efforts. They write for producers. What moves them to write is the picture they envision of their painstaking work brought to life on the stage—and the greatest inducement that can be offered them is an honorable production.

It is the producers, then, who set the standard. If we want fine plays, let us not say to our authors, "We can only afford six actors and cannot build an ambitious set." Let us say, "Give us your best, and we will meet your requirements."

Regretfully, English-speaking countries have few producers in a position to say this. Yet, if we are to build a literature of real consequence, it must be said. Children's-theatre producers, of all others, must be brave enough to dream an impossible dream—and practical enough to make it come true.

"Warriors Dance" from *Kojo and the Leopard* directed by Kelsey E. Collie.
Choreography by Muriel Burwell.

Kelsey E. Collie is Associate Professor of Drama and Producing-Director
of the Howard University Children's Theatre. He is a graduate of Hamp-
ton Institute, holds his M.F.A. degree from George Washington University, and is a Ph.D. candidate at Howard.

Professor Collie has written a number of plays for his theatre and has
had a play, a short story, and articles published. He is a member of the
American Theatre Association and is presently vice-president and presi-
dent-elect of its Black Theatre Program. He is also a member of the Children's Theatre Association of America; the National Society of Arts and
Letters; and the American Association of University Professors. He was
recipient of the 1974 Winifred Ward Award, presented by the CTAA.
Collie is listed in *Who's Who in the Southwest, Who's Who among Black Americans, Men of Achievement,* and *Dictionary of International Biographies.*

THE DEVELOPMENT OF A BLACK CHILDREN'S THEATRE: A BEGINNING

6

KELSEY E. COLLIE

Theatregoing among black Americans is not a long-standing tradition. Except for some well-to-do few or a somewhat limited group of arts followers, theatre was considered a luxury, not financially but culturally. Television since its inception and motion pictures before that had relegated blacks to minor roles, often uncomplimentary ones. Further, the life-styles portrayed in the films were not relevant to blacks. In other words, the American dream and the American dreamers were neither attainable nor reflective of the masses of Afro-Americans.

Since the 1960s, however, it has become increasingly apparent that the theatre is a tremendous vehicle for entertainment, educational enrichment, and propaganda. In the Sixties Imamu Baraka (LeRoi Jones), Ron Milner, and Ed Bullins reached the peak of their popularity. Theatre helped to crystallize, clarify, and dramatize many of the issues of the black revolution. It focused on some of the problems with which blacks were faced, and it called for action (in some instances), while at the same time providing a few hours of entertainment.

The success of the black-theatre movement in the United States during the Sixties marked the beginning of a new cultural outlet. No longer were blacks assigned to onstage roles as maids, butlers, and varied buffoons. Now black playwrights could draw characters who, though sometimes appearing larger than life, were far more authentic to black audiences than were some previous types.

For the most part, however, the plays developed during that period were primarily intended for adult audiences. None could be strictly categorized as children's theatre, and, despite the argument by some black playwrights that their plays were intended for all black people—"we have to teach black folk from an early age to prepare themselves for survival in this country"— few parents exposed their children to them. They felt the plays were not suitable in content or language for young, impressionable minds.

As a matter of fact, except for the schools and some few theatre groups across the country, black children witnessed little theatre and even less good quality productions. Unless a local or touring children's-theatre group performed, there was no live theatre for black children. Again, the subject matter and images projected onstage were not always acceptable to either children or their parents.

The need, then, for solid, pertinent theatre experiences for black children became quite clear. The usefulness of theatre as an educational tool looms even larger now as educators attempt to discover innovative methods of teaching not only reading, writing, and arithmetic but also the mores, customs, and cultural heritage of Afro-Americans. Through the sheer fantasy that is theatre and the joy that is inherent in children's theatre, black children today are being exposed to an art form that can and will provide them with an appreciation for life that was not afforded many of their parents.

An ever-increasing interest in a theatre that speaks to the needs of Afro-American children is evidenced by the further development and growth of children's theatres in Cleveland, Ohio; Compton, California; New York City; Houston, Texas; Knoxville, Tennessee; Atlanta, Georgia; San Diego, California; Milwaukee, Wisconsin; Boston, Massachusetts; New Orleans, Louisiana; and Washington, D.C. The fact that scripts providing positive images and themes relevant to blacks are, at this juncture, scarce does not dishearten producers and directors. Many still use the classical fairy tales or other tried and proven works as their mainstays. However, it is apparent that not until black playwrights take children's theatre seriously and begin writing for it, and producers concern themselves with quality and germane themes, will a truly black children's theatre evolve. That black producers and performers provide audiences with productions of *Hello, Dolly!*, *Hamlet*, or *Guys and Dolls* does not make them a truly black production. Cinderella or Snow White may embody universal messages, but do they provide positive images for young blacks to emulate? Are the experiences from a black culture and tradition? Are the problems posed and the solutions offered from a black perspective?

Children's theatre is a business—a worthwhile business. Unless it is the university-based theatre or some similar institution that is underwritten by a parent organization that can absorb production costs, the commercial children's theatre must depend on its box-office returns if it expects to subsist. Certainly, children's theatre does not compete with adult or more family-oriented theatres. And rightly, it should not. Theatre should be accessible to all people: this is most important for children's theatre. If it is not financially within the reach of the masses, it may become a luxury—attended and therefore supported only by an economically elite group.

A black children's theatre should be central to the lives of all black people—adults, adolescents, and children. It should not be so limited that only a restricted audience can enjoy it or want to see it. Perhaps it would be better to call this form of theatrical production "family theatre," but that might lead to the kind of rating distinctions subscribed to by the motion-picture industry. Those ratings have created more problems than they have solved.

What is being advocated here is nothing new. Parents and older brothers and sisters have been taking younger children to the theatre for quite some time. Why, then, shouldn't the theatre take this into account and produce the kind of dramatic production that can be enjoyed by any age level? Good theatre is good no matter for what age it is being presented.[1] If it isn't good, then why should anyone bother producing it?

Black children's theatre should strive for wide audience appeal. Resident theatres and touring companies ought to perform plays that meet the needs of a large segment of the theatregoing population. Theatre managers cannot turn back parents at the doors of the theatres and forbid their entrance. By the same token, to deny entrance to a child under six is to

1. For the purpose of this discussion the term "good" indicates a suitable worth attributed to the quality of a production dictated by a standard value judgment.

deny all children the right to behold and enjoy an experience that cannot be duplicated by television or motion pictures. Some three- and four-year-olds have sat in a theatre thoroughly fascinated by what they saw unfold before their very eyes. At a performance of a play supposedly designed for under twelves, a fifteen-year-old was observed shrieking and hiding from an actor dressed in a leopard's costume. Another example of the wide appeal some children's plays have for audiences was made known at a production that featured a young girl who had a speech problem and the adventures she encounters while overcoming her problem. A mother of three who had brought her children to see the production the first time returned a second time with her husband in tow. She reported that they "loved it!" The ear-to-ear smile on her husband's face supported the woman's remark.

These are examples of only a few of the kinds of people who attend shows designed for children. Theatre managers, producers, playwrights, designers, and performers must be aware that they are being observed and critiqued by persons in all age ranges and with varied experience. They must be aware that the theatre must meet a person at a particular level and move to yet another, higher level. It is questionable whether the theatre experience that is unileveled is worthy of production. For black audiences, a play that does not take its playgoers beyond the point at which they began the experience is not a beneficial one. For children, especially, that higher level should be in terms of educating them to theatre in general, to universal truths, and more specifically to black life-styles.

Without sermonizing, theatre can preach;[2] without a sledgehammer it can be polemical; without being excessive or heavy-handed it can be a tool for propaganda. There is nothing innovative, revolutionary, or militant about this approach to theatre. It has all been done in America for many years and for centuries in Europe.

There is room in black children's theatre for traditional materials treated traditionally. Here again it is not the fairy tale to which this discussion refers. *Peter Pan* and *Alice in Wonderland* are traditional and may be performed, but these should not be considered black simply because they are produced by blacks. Where feasible, the more traditional form may be considered as a last resort. *The Wiz,* though not in the purest sense a play for children, is an example of a traditional play given an updated, uptempoed treatment with an ethnic flavor. This kind of production comes closer

2. This is not to say that sermons should not be utilized, for important themes have often been expressed through hard-hitting sermons such as Dr. Martin Luther King's "I Have a Dream" speech or the sermons found in James Weldon Johnson's *God's Trombones.*

to what black children's theatre should be. However, it too lacks all the qualities essential to make it aesthetically, culturally, and artistically a black theatre piece.

Today's urban black child is often faced with numerous problems— more than his white counterpart. How does this child manage to cope? The theatre can help to resolve these problems and also to allay fears that the child is alone in facing a particular crisis. Children today are concerned with divorce, adoption, death, old age, environmental pollution, birth control, religious beliefs, and sex. Are they to be denied reasonable solutions, tastefully and visually presented on stage? These topics are dealt with in adult theatre, so why shouldn't children's theatre deal with them on a level understandable to children?

This is not to say that all the material for the child audience should be concerned with heavy topics. On the contrary. For despite the fact that many black children must cope with problems of day-to-day survival in the inner city, it does not mean that they need have the theatre reflect only the sordid, problematic, and often unpleasant segments of their lives. There is joy and celebration in the black child's life, and not to reflect this in the drama portrayed on stage is to do what television and motion pictures have done consistently and successfully. For all the "Good Times" and "The Jeffersons" there are the in-betweeners. These are the people whose stories rarely are heard or seen. "Julia," late of television, was not the answer; *Cooley High* comes closer, and so does *Sounder.* For all the Superflys and superstuds proudly presented on the super 35-mm screen, there are has-beens and common, quite ordinary folk who wear Sears suits, Kinney shoes, and eat at Kentucky Fried Chicken regularly. They feel important to themselves, and that can make for interesting theatre, especially for young blacks who must face the reality that they will more than likely never get to be Jim Brown, Ron O'Neil, Tamara Dobson, or Jim Kelly. Reality can be harsh sometimes. Black children's theatre should be about the business of providing positive images for youth to emulate. It should once and for all erase the mythical and stereotypical from the stage. Let the motion pictures have their larger-than-life heroes who karate-chop their way through reel after reel of blood-and-guts macho make-believe in their leather suits and velvet-lined chartreuse Porsches. The stage can do without it.

Fertile areas for scripts can be found in the folk tales of Africa, the West Indies, and the United States. Children's books written by new young black authors are other sources of material. Sharon Bell Mathis and Eloise Greenfield are two of the most prolific. More established writers such as Gwendolyn Brooks and Ann Petry also have fine offerings. But for the creative company that wants to do its own thing, the script developed jointly by a playwright, director, and actors provides a reward well worth the effort. Certainly the benefits to all concerned are numerous. However, the one that will probably mean the most is that which comes from an audience response and the fact that each member of the company recognizes that he or she has been instrumental in creating the final product.

Who makes up that creative company is unimportant. That the child audience is not neglected is the primary concern. Of course, this does not mean that quality and good taste are sacrificed. They are foremost to the mounting of any show; but whether professionals, amateurs, students, children, or a combination of some or all of these, the first requisite is that they all honestly believe in what they are doing. Children need and deserve honesty in the theatre, even when they understand that they are being titillated by a fascinating script, attractive sets and costumes, and adroit actors.

Believability comes through, whether a show is on a street corner, behind a proscenium arch, or in the round. Black children's theatre needs all these performing spaces for exploration and experimentation. Just as no one space will satisfy all the needs of this theatre, so no one production style can or should satisfy. There is merit in participation plays, story theatre, and the musical. The form is merely the vehicle by which the story is told. One form may best suit a particular play, while another may not. Performers, directors, and writers ought to experiment with several forms before they lock themselves into one form or another.

Whatever the style, whatever the content, theatre for black children must provide the young theatregoer with positive images, relevant themes, and quality productions. There can be no compromise about these. Along with these elements must go the marriage of education and entertainment. Simply having one without the other is not constructive in the development of a black children's theatre. Finally, many traditional and classical plays must be discarded to make room for innovative, contemporary pieces.

It is not sufficient for the theatre to compete with television and motion pictures; it must outstrip them both. The impact of the stage is greater than either of the aforementioned media, and, if utilized properly, theatre can become the greatest means for reform that this country has ever witnessed.

Children's theatre should be made accessible to all children. White children can gain from viewing a show primarily designed for blacks. As much as blacks need to improve self-image, this same expression needs to be shown to others, who may also learn and thereby make corrections of any cultural misinterpretations or misgivings they may have harbored.

Children are a part of the great adventure known as life. Whether they realize it or not, they are a part of the history that is being written daily. Black children have a heritage, culture, tradition, and more, which have been passed down through the ages from generation to generation and from continent to continent, country to country. Black children need to be reminded of these, shown these, and asked to respond to them. Only then can they feel that they have a stake in their heritage; only then will they begin to see and appreciate the beauty and joy that is theatre. Only then will theatregoing become a part of their life-style. It is a challenge offered producers, one that has been accepted. This is only a beginning, but what a marvelous beginning!

The Little Match Girl conceived and directed by John Clark Donahue for the Children's Theatre Company, Minneapolis.

John Clark Donahue is Artistic Director of the Children's Theatre Company of Minneapolis. He holds degrees in Art Education and Theatre from the University of Minnesota. In 1962 he became director and designer, writer and teacher for the Moppet Players, an organization that three years later became affiliated with the Minneapolis Institute of the Arts. Under Donahue's leadership the Children's Theatre Company has evolved a unique ensemble approach to production. Plays based on original scripts have been toured throughout the Midwest and into Washington, D.C., Connecticut, New York, and Canada.

In 1970 the Rockefeller Foundation awarded this group the largest grant ever given to a company performing for children. The CTC has made a ninety-minute film that has received highly favorable notices, and two collections of its plays are now available. Donahue's work, in addition to an emphasis on originality of expression, holds the educational objective that "theatre should be a vital, creative working center, providing a multifaceted art environment for the young person as well as the professional artist."

In 1974 the company moved into its new facilities in the $4.5 million theatre/classroom building in the Minneapolis Fine Arts Park. Here a company of artists is being formed for the purpose of producing both classical and experimental works.

7　　　　TELL ME THINGS

JOHN CLARK DONAHUE

*A*s a teacher of children, I want to help bring the child into the real world. As a maker of plays, I want to bring theatre for children into the real world. I am working to relate and integrate efforts in the field of children's theatre to the functions and significance of theatre as a whole.

I fear, however, that a great deal of what is perceived to be the significance of theatre is revealed in our attitude toward children's theatre. If we thought that the experience of theatre was a truly powerful and meaningful aspect of our lives, we wouldn't treat theatre for children as lightly as we seem to. Obviously, theatre in general is not seen as very important, except as it exists as a function of amusement and a social institution.

In the same way, we do not think of our children as significant members of our society—our real world. We don't want them entering that domain, and we resent their attempts to do so. We want to isolate them and maintain them as they are and deny their efforts to leave a state of being that exists only in our own adult minds and has no corresponding reality in fact. I believe this is because we feel guilt concerning our own processes of growing up, and for that reason we try to prevent our children from going through the same thing. We try to keep them in little-child capsules or child suits, with limited vocabulary and sheltered experience. And then suddenly —snap—at age eighteen they are supposed to be grown up. Or at a certain point we begin to make jokes about what they're doing behind the barn.

I've always sensed in the children that I come in contact with continually —and from very strong memories of my own childhood—the desire to become whole, to grow and mature and discover and to be allowed to participate in the process of discovery that children perceive to be going on around them. If we are vulnerable as adults, we will admit to that process and invite our children to participate with us.

One of the most wonderful things that you can do for your own child is to invite him to discover *with you* every new thing—pathways, the eating of drippy fruit, running together, rolling down a hill, crying—every significant life experience. I can think of no more beautiful vision than a circle of people—grandmothers and fathers and mothers and babies and young adults and teenagers and small children—gathered around a fire late at night, all holding one another and swaying, the wrinkled faces and the smooth young faces all giving over to something more primal and universally felt, and all of them simply celebrating the different rings on a tree.

The opportunities for such a communion among the human family are far more rare today than they used to be. Grandmother no longer lives in our home until she dies. The midwife no longer comes to our house to deliver the baby in the presence of the entire family. Our children no longer work side by side with us in the fields or in the shop, sharing responsibilities and receiving first hand the knowledge and experience of their elders. Even in church the children are now sent off into a separate room to hear some watered-down version of what their parents—sitting in the real church—give every indication of not understanding themselves. We are all of us isolated from one another.

I believe that one means of restoring this broken communion exists—potentially at least—in theatre.

I want to talk about a type of audience I call *normal,* as opposed to *abnormal,* audience groups. By this I mean a gathering composed of the kind of mix in ages, backgrounds, and interests that one encounters in normal, day-to-day life rather than a particular stratum or select assemblage. By this definition an abnormal audience is one which, for instance, consists exclusively of adult theatregoers or exclusively of eight-year-old Cub Scouts and Brownies—in other words, just the type of stratified group that is taken for granted when one speaks of theatre and children's theatre.

During the past fifteen years of our work in the Minneapolis Children's Theatre Company and School we have come close to evolving a *normal* audience, so that when I talk about my work in children's theatre I am actually talking about how I tell stories, for example, to eight-year-olds, their parents, teenagers, senior citizens, adults who have no children, executives, blue-collar workers, theatregoers, and nontheatregoers. There has been generated here a tremendous *mix.*

Some of my own works may *mean* something only when seen by a mix of audience. *Hang On To Your Head* does not work if seen by children only or adults only. It is a message to parents as well as children, and it's in the mixed emotions and perceptions of a mixed audience that much of our work derives its power.

So what does children's theatre become in this context? What is mutually appealing to this heterogenous gathering? I believe that the things of childhood stay with us. Somehow it seems to me that if we think children's theatre is a good thing for our children—and indeed for us—it's because we think it will have something to do with those sensations and perceptions and feelings and involvements of our collective childhoods.

What are these? The discovery of the color red. The smell of mud or moss. The sudden flutter of a lot of birds. The mysterious glance of a pair of eyes through a hedge. Grapevines going up the side of Grandfather's porch. A red-dotted bug disocvered working its way through a leaf structure. The voices of leprechauns. And statues. And the belief in it all that we somehow have as children.

Maybe children's theatre, defined in this way, has to do with celebrating all these mysteries. If some people view it as teaching lessons or as propoganda, they would be right in thinking that young minds are open and fresh and formative. But I would like to think of it as a place in the community where all these profound and mysterious things that children *know* are affirmed and rejoiced over instead of denied or made to seem of little worth. And I would like to think of it as that place in the community where, for older people, these sensations, remembrances, vague associations, and deeply felt emotions—which have never died—can be returned to. Referred to. Shared. In a communion that brings children and adults together and makes them one.

One night I was talking with Ben Blackhawk, a student in the Children's Theatre School. A group of staff members and boys and girls from the Theatre Company were spending the night in the woods outside Minneapolis, where they had been performing *commedia dell'arte* for a local festival. It was late, and the talk was quiet. Except for the stars, the only light came from a few scattered candles. The fourteen-year-old suddenly turned to me and said, "*Tell* me things."

Children *want* things from adults. It's best to let them ask for them or to offer them in ways that are not too threatening. Which means that we should be able to offer them parables, tales, magic, visions, games that will allow the child to step into the depths of waters at the child's rate. If we ourselves are truly vulnerable and fearless, our children are going to feel that and learn from us.

Some children learn to be untruthful very early on. They use their parents' behavior as a model. We say that children are not deceived, but many of them are led down the wrong path. They do grow up to be their parents—carbon copies and worse.

I think that what we teach our children in terms of fear—of what to fear —is, of course, a revelation of what we ourselves fear. And that extends from teaching them not to eat certain foods (think of an adult who has never eaten a mango, for instance, telling his child in the supermarket not to be silly when the child eagerly comes up to him bearing a mango) to teaching them that there is no God.

I always try to tell children not to be afraid. That's different from telling them that the stove is hot, of course. I say, "The stove is hot. You can touch it if you want to. You'll burn your finger. If you want to know what a burn is like, then touch it." Well, they don't touch it then because they know that they're able to and that I would allow them to be burned.

I am depressed by children's-theatre people who are still asking each other at conventions, "What do you make your mushrooms out of—crepe paper or cardboard?" It's like listening to a group of people comparing potato-salad recipes—a group of people, none of whom make very good potato salad—but who luxuriate in saying, "Do you use sweet pickle juice or dill pickle in yours?"

Children want to become like water, like birds; they want somehow to be pure and harmonious and exquisite. And then sometimes they want to be like a horned toad. They want to be ugly. In my play, *Old Kieg of Malfi*, a very pretty girl—who all her life has been beautiful and has had to carry the burden of beauty—says, "Oh, I want to be as ugly as an old stink pot toad. And then I would walk up to my mother and my teacher and say, 'How do I look? I'm ready to be married.'" And then the girl is miraculously given a hideously ugly toad mask. She is given the opportunity to be ugly. Which is a great gift.

I feel that one of my tasks is to give a child the chance to transform into an ugly witch, an ugly toad, and to be evil. Because, as we all know, if we're not allowed to be evil—not allowed to let that side of us come out—it's eventually going to emerge in ways that are awful and destructive. Or else it will be bottled up forever and never admitted to, which is another lie. I think a lot of the old tales that have to do with bottles or vessels or lamps are actually about that.

The child is not wanted in certain places at certain times. And he is not wanted there because we feel guilty about having a child see and hear what we do and say. We perceive the child to be a pure side of ourselves—or relatively pure, because the child has his dark side—and we do not want him to be around to observe certain aspects of our behavior. The child may point up our lies and see the truth of who we are. Perhaps in the case of fairy tales, myths, legends, and make-believe, we can find safety. Perhaps this is why so much is learned and discussed in great depth—potentially—in the telling of those tales. Maybe that's the way lessons can be passed on and learned without threat to us.

The tales are not about you or me but people who lived a long time ago. They provide a safe way of telling our children that, yes, we do lie, we do murder—yes, we do all these things. And of course the child understands.

The ancient tales are so complex and profound that they require the utmost skill and artistry to reveal their life—that which has preserved them and passed them down through the years, with mystery and meaning intact. One can seldom strike that magic. One gathers together the best people one can and then simply tries to make theatre pieces, either from impulse or as a homage to something that exists and is beautiful and important.

I cannot view the story alone. I can't imagine anything more senseless. Of course, some stories are so powerful that they can be told well anywhere, under any circumstances—in basements in front of bedspreads. But even then the true power is in the telling—in finding a story's truth and believing it and making a gift of it to others. To discover the power of transformation does not necessarily require a lot of lights and scenery, but it does take a real *giving over*—and then it suddenly all becomes very mysterious.

The people who come to our theatre in Minneapolis do not ultimately come to hear the stories. In a sense they come for the *telling*.

Do the part where you kick your heels, Grandpa. Grandma, do the part where you stand up and quack!

The stories are known, most of them by heart. But they are either told well—that is, truthfully—or they are a lie. The actual moment and manner of the telling are all-important and transfiguring.

And so it goes with Grandma and Marceau and the Brothers Grimm and all the legendary priests of transportation and transformation. If we have a good storyteller in our village, we take pride in him and want to protect him and depend on him. And we go to him *with* our children. The children, of course, run ahead to get the best seats in front.

The old stories are as wondrously modern as can be and have a tremendous power and significance for a modern audience. But then—I keep repeating myself—it's all in the telling. You have to discover what the tales are about and find a way to bring them alive.

An anthology of three of my plays received bad reviews from an academic journal. The reviewer said they were "not theatrical" and "certainly not for children." Not for children? If that's the case, none of the fairy tales —if viewed objectively—are for children, because they're farther out than anything I've created. What is for children? So many things are absolutely essential to a child's development—an admission and understanding of the pain and punishment, the failures, the ecstasy—all so important for a child to get through life.

What's different about writing a play for children and writing a play for adults? I offer to children the things that are precious and meaningful to *me* and that are wonderful and mysterious to *me*. At the same time, I don't write about things that children aren't interested in. I think a lot of adult work is very limited in its scope—such as a play about the problems of divorce or about a *menage á trois*. These things articulate adult neurotic concerns in a way that is very specific. These themes are not as universal and ancient as the stuff of fairy tales. These matters are dealt with in fairy tales and children's legends—psychological, sexual, religious concerns— but they are played out on a grand scale and enveloped in a kind of wonderful mystery that allows them to be felt in a mysterious way by a child audience. They are not so explicit and didactic and laid out as, for instance, stories by Jacqueline Susann, or even "The Honeymooners." Children may not be interested in Thornton's Wilder's *The Matchmaker* because they're not involved in the machinations of marriage or leaving their work to go to the city or anything like that. They are interested in grand things, such as life and death, discovery, in growing older. They are interested in sex but in the same way as they are interested in birth and dying—as an element of life. They are not interested in what went wrong with sex or other such adult matters.

They are very interested in love, in the giving and caring involved with love. They are much aware of the security of the womb. They applaud with great pleasure in *The Little Match Girl* when she is united with her grand-mother and ascends into heaven. They are more eager to celebrate her ascension than to mourn her death. After our production of *The Little Match Girl* some of the children asked me why no one stopped to help the freezing child, and I always answered—despite the fact that they all knew the answer—"That's the way it is. We don't have enough love in the world to care for one another as completely as we should."

We are not needed by our children, except when we are needed. Which is one of the great things we must learn as parents and as adults working with and caring for children. We need one another in certain ways and at certain times, and we have to be able to perceive that subtle structure of things. There are moments when we need one another deeply and times when we do not want to be grabbed at.

People say, "Oh, God, let's get away from the children." And that *is* necessary. I think it's possible to create a situation whereby our children know that we need a certain amount of time alone, apart from them. And through an understanding of the security of mutual love, they will come to interpret that need and will simply be gone, so that parents can be together as beautiful, loving children as well. But the ability to create such an atmosphere—listen to me ramble all over the place—probably has to do with not having guilt.

In *Old Kieg of Malfi* I tried to depict a whole society that could not bear to think that it was no longer needed. That symptom, or syndrome, was depicted in the character of the loving and lovely Mrs. Souss, the old housekeeper. I was writing about America and its inability to give way to a new generation, to give up almost everything that it has accomplished in order to be reborn. I was, perhaps, pessimistic about the specific nation at that specific time but optimistic about the nature of mankind—optimistic because of a vision I believe is recurrent throughout literature: the image of the child, the little boy sitting alone amid the desolation of the universe, who is glimpsed out of the window in the closing moments of Beckett's *Endgame,* a play that is ultimately optimistic, in my opinion. In *Old Kieg of Malfi* the old wizard evaporates but leaves behind his cap and gown, which are taken up anew by a child, so that the "old Kieg" simply *comes back.* Mrs. Souss, who could not bear the letting go, mails herself away to the dead-letter office, and hers is the tragedy.

We hate very much to think that what we have created is no longer viable, to think that a part of us—our children—may no longer need us. Instead of celebrating that freedom—that part of us that is moving out to create anew and to discover anew—we attempt to hold our children back. In the same way, what I perceive in so much of theatre is a desperate hanging on instead of a casting off—a joyous statement that we have nothing, we don't know where we're going, but we're going —we have faith and we're *going.*

When I'm asked what forms to use when making theatre for children, I try to talk about what I understand of the child-perception. I know that the child's ability to leap from place to place, from time to time, to transform age, sex, species, to move from one plane to another—from earth to never-land or whatever—is very great. Children do it all the time; it's simply a part of their living process. So that means that the forms we develop or choose in theatre for young people are limitless. When I teach children, when I work with children, when I sit with them in a circle and tell tales, they're able to follow wherever I go, with total ease. And their ability to make abstract connections is total. The way Jonathan Winters used to take a coat hanger or a ruler and make all those things happen with it—children know that so completely. And that means that you can tell a story to a child in any way. Just tell it truthfully.

At the same time, people question me about my use of naturalistic or realistic stage settings, as opposed to what is called "leaving it to the children's imaginations." In telling the story of *Treasure Island,* you can take a

board and a pole and have it be the *Hispaniola,* or you can built a fully
outfitted ship. Both of them will work, but in different ways. Both of them
will get to the island. The latter method, however, may have to do with
some acknowledgment of theatre history and the development of tale-
telling—and some of the work that I do is done in a deliberately old-
fashioned manner because it does acknowledge a time when a certain style
was very appealing and popular. And I happen to think that that grand
style always remains appealing. I believe that a large section of the population loves spectacle and wants to say, "Gee, that boat looked real." "Gee,
that tree looked like a tree." Which they know it didn't, but it did.

I think it's possible that adults who are tied to that kind of perception in
their own lives—requiring a very specific delineation and articulation—and
who don't share the child's ability to make abstract connections may feel
purged and freed when they see work done in quite the opposite way.
They respond to it as being fresh and childlike. They may look at a child
swinging in an inner tube and saying, "See—I'm a bird" and think of that as
heady food and liberating and therapeutic. But I think that most children,
as they make do with a board and a pole, would actually rather be sailing
one of the "tall ships."

I don't think that naturalistic spectacle is by any means the only way of
telling stories to children, and I do not use it exclusively in my own work.
But I do know that it is a valid way of making things materialize at one end
of a room, in a theatre. People say, "Oh, it's too elaborate. Children don't
need it, children don't want it." I feel that children may not need it, but
they certainly do appreciate it when it's offered to them. I don't think that
everything should be reduced to colored boxes and cardboard circles. In
Paul Klee's paintings, which are praised for their wonderful childlike naïv-
etè, there is an extraordinary complexity and mystery that is far more
complicated than a N.C. Wyeth illustration of *Treasure Island* or *The
Deerslayer.*

I should say, in the midst of these observations and statements of belief,
that I may not have any answers for anybody else. I am able to speak only
about my own experience and the very specific chemistry we have built up
during the fifteen years that have formed the Minneapolis Children's
Theatre Company and School. And perhaps our specific situation, our
methods and philosophies—like certain wines and cheeses—may not travel
very well. They may not be applicable elsewhere, under different circumstances and with different chemistries. I only know what I see and understand in my own community, and that's all that is important to me. What
we're doing here may not fit others' needs, and I'm not sure that it should.

I urge people to make theatre wherever they are, in their own way, and
to surround themselves with as many skillful tellers of all kinds—musicians,

dancers, and so on—as are available to tell the tales. And I hope they will have something worthy to tell, to speak of, to share with the young, because they are eager to hear. And if you tell it well enough, the children will be happy to return over and over again to the place of inspiration and mystery.

Before you can make anything to share with anybody, you have to like yourself and trust your own vision. In order to dare to share that some-thing you have to feel one of at least three things: You must have a sense that you have some kind of receptive community, so that what you set forth is not trampled on or chewed up. Or you have to be striking out angrily because you feel you're doomed anyway. Or you have to be in an almost trancelike state, a mystical state of being, which is, in a sense, the most pure. One's conscious perception, then, is not of any significance at all. Instead, one participates in a ceremony of communion with one's self and others in the group art of theatre—a ceremony that is fulfilling for the group and then is simply shared with those who wish to come and see it. In that case, you just tack up a sign that says, "It's here." That's most appealing to me, but things aren't often that pure.

Generally, one's ability to make theatre successfully—and to make theatre for children—is not only dependent on one's artistic resources. It depends on one's audience in almost equal measure. But audiences—per-haps especially in the case of what we're calling children's theatre—can be developed and nurtured and embraced. We can assist them, through our work, to *complete* that community or communion that is our reason for existence.

If we've done anything to bring children's theatre closer to the center of theatrical energy and creation and focus, it's because adults as well as children have been moved and impressed with the total effect of certain works they have seen. If it's good for me, then it must be good for my children. If I'm moved by something or learn a lesson or perceive a truth, then I want that to be shared with my child. I want to be a part of it. I want my child to be a part of it. Together we want to be part of it all as audience. Because what has happened to me while there has been positive.

The decision made by the adult as to what is "good for" the child has to do with what has happened to that adult person. The adults are participat-ing themselves—and not merely vicariously through their children. The child in this context is not isolated from the theatrical experience, but the community is brought in to see certain works in a certain *mix* that is not experienced elsewhere. This richness of mix in our audiences contributes immeasurably to the experience of all who participate—children, adults, and artists.

I know that children deeply appreciate the presence of adults, the mothers and fathers and grandparents, because they respond differently to the works when they are there. Children's behavior is more reverent—and not out of fear of being scolded for improper behavior but out of a thankfulness and awareness that this is a more real coming together than occurs when their peer group is herded in to scream and shout in a ritual way on a Thursday morning.

Adults *use* the children's plays. They feel able to give a greater portion of themselves to the work because they feel they're somehow free from harm. They bring their children to the plays, and that in turn gives them the freedom to be vulnerable. It isn't for them; it's for the children, they say. But in the darkness they can give love to their children and to the players and to one another in the audience in a way that is very difficult for most in our society in the context of adult theatre.

As an artist, one tries to give a gift to people whom one respects and loves—but the giving becomes possible only through their willingness to receive. That's all I can do as an artist of the theatre: observe and attempt to understand and then share my understandings with people who are willing to look and listen.

Children *want* things from adults. As a teacher of children, I know that one of the things that delights them most is any manifestation of their own nature that I exhibit: tying pans to my feet and running down the hall—we should *all* do that. Let's allow the children to teach us how important that sort of behavior—the constant revival of our own child-souls—is to maintaining our sanity, our wholeness.

At the same time, children want me to be an adult. They depend on me to fulfill certain adult functions; they want me to see to certain things that they do not have the desire or inclination to do. I have the ability to create possibilities for them that they will learn to participate in without knowing the how or the why of it.

So, as a child, you fetch the grain and you help till and you sometimes ask why, but a lot of the time you just enjoy the pleasure of the doing. And leave the why and the how for later.

One offers children both, and they accept a balance between the delight they have in the child-antics and madness of adults on one hand, and the occasions of deep reverence, commitment and grave thought on the other. Children have time for both.

I make theatre for children because of the significance that the child has for me—as a force, a life force that guides and enlightens. We must continually look to the child for guidance as well as helping to guide the child. If we do so, we will discover a unity among us and a wholeness—a dimension of ourselves that I find missing in the cold, frightened, calculating, and lying worlds that I see around me. If we're not quite sure where we're at, then we should look to the child—but by that I also mean we should look to the child *in us*. And that is the part of our lives with which we seem to be so out of touch.

It may be that in childhood our center or soul (I use the word "center" for those who are made uncomfortable by the word "soul") shines forth more clearly. And as we grow older, if we're not careful and if we're not treated with care, that center tends to be submerged. But the child is a part of our wholeness as we mature and must not be discarded. If the child is the purest manifestation of the spiritual center or light in us—and I feel that strongly—then we must always put ourselves close to the child as teacher. Christ in the temple.

Let us create a *place*. Let us create a place in our communities that, in turn, will help generate a genuine *community*.

As long as we don't seem to be taking our children with us to *Oedipus Rex* —and that is one play our children should be able to share with us—then let us go with them to a place that is covered by the term "children's theatre." If we don't take them to see *Who's Afraid of Virginia Woolf?*, maybe it's because we're afraid they'll see us in those characters. All right. Then let's go with them to see some things in which we are all free from harm and accusing fingers, because of the dimension, the remove, and the fantastic configurations of the tales we will hear there.

Get people who are artists and people of the theatre and people of mystery and get the town in—the community—and tell tales that aren't being told anywhere else. Let's not talk there about a specific war or a specific rape or a specific this or that but talk about the more ancient rhythms, pebbles, tree barks, howls that concern us all. There ought to be a theatre in each town of any size that does that. And it's marvelous to call it "children's theatre" because who *would* we want to hear the important stories—if we want to plant the seeds of concern—more than our children?

But we must be there with them, so that together we create a chemistry and a communion that makes the event meaningful and as deep as the subject matter. We will only perceive it to be deep if our gathering and our giving are meaningful. And that is what I see as the significance of children's theatre.

PART III

The Presentation: Performance and Production

From Orlin Corey's production of *Reynard the Fox.*

In the field of children's theatre **Orlin Corey** is well known as a producer, actor, writer, publisher, and lecturer. He holds two degrees from Baylor University and has studied at the University of Kentucky, the Central School of Speech and Drama in London, the University of London, and the Louvre. In 1949 he married Irene Lockridge, an artist and costume designer. As founders and co-producers of the Everyman Players, they developed a professional company dedicated to the staging of visually exciting pageants and plays that could be enjoyed and understood by children as well as adults. For over a decade they toured their productions of *The Book of Job, The Pilgrim's Progress, The Tempest, Reynard the Fox, The Tortoise and the Hare,* and other classics to all parts of the United States, Venice, London, Santiago, and a number of cities in South Africa.

The Coreys have been presented with the Religious Drama Award of the National Catholic Theatre Conference, a special award from the New England Theatre Conference, and the Jennie Heiden Award from the American Theatre Association.

Orlin Corey was president of the Children's Theatre Association of America from 1971 to 1973. In 1977 Mr. Corey became publisher-editor of the Anchorage Press.

"GO, MAKE READY"

8

A Philosophy of Making
Theatre for Children*

ORLIN COREY

*T*hose words of Hamlet quoted in the title of this article were addressed to the players. In "making ready" there is and should be great diversity. Therefore I shall eschew "upper case" theories that always ring with authority, for they breed disciples and skeptics in almost equal proportion. I distrust both. My choice is a "lower case" statement of my personal philosophy of producing plays for children as it seems to me today.

My own phrase perturbs me. To "produce plays for children" seems so pretentious. I am reminded of Arthur Ransome's statement about children's books: "I do not know how to write books for children and have the greatest doubts as to whether anybody should try to do any such thing. . . . You write not for children but for yourself, and if, by good fortune, children enjoy what you enjoy, why then, you are a writer of children's books . . . . No special credit to you, but simply thumping good luck."

Even that good word "children" is suspect. In medieval times it meant the descendants of the clan or race. Today it is one of the shrinking terms in a society that is anxious to remain young and less than responsible. I would use the word "children" in this older, larger sense as descendants of the race. They are the original audience of theatre. Theirs is a virginal awareness of the adventure of living. To make theatre for them is a privi-

* An address to the annual conference of Region Five of the Children's Theatre Conference meeting in San Antonio in 1968. The general subject was requested by the program committee.

lege and a challenge. They inherit a tradition they neither know nor understand, for, in America, the past is as novel as tomorrow.*

It is a cliché of our profession that theatre for children is a lesser achievement, an easier assignment because mediocre work will go unnoticed. I find this a doubly shameful attitude. It condemns the one who believes it, and those who believe it jauntily perpetrate theatrical crimes, ignorantly insulting two audiences—today's and tomorrow's. The only distinction I would make between theatre for children and theatre for adults is that for children it must be better. Not all adult theatre will engage the attention of children, but theatre good enough to earn the attention of children will entertain an adult.

Theatre for children must be truer. That is, it must belong to the universals of mankind, whereas adult theatre may properly limit itself to the emotional casualties of an age, such as Blanche DuBois, in *A Streetcar Named Desire* or the spiritual cripples of society, such as Willy Loman, in *Death of a Salesman* or tortured victims of marriage and choice, such as George and Martha in *Who's Afraid of Virginia Woolf?* Adult theatre may be preoccupied with pessimism, though this is a dull diet if unvaried for men who must bend their bodies against the earth for survivial. A mood of doubt may be appropriate to an age, and to disregard that reality would be false to the very life the theatre exists to mirror. Hugh Hunt of the Australian Elizabethan Theatre Trust once observed: "Pessimism is not an enduring human theme." Theatre for our descendants must not merely bequeath our despair, for there is no legacy in doubt. Theatre for our youthful life requires a longer look, one that does not ignore the potential nobility of man amid his ignobility. To despair of man's ability to survive his own evil is to deny the adventure of our long existence.

Theatre for children, intrinsically more adventurous and theatrical, requires high performance and production achievement indeed. High standards are demanded by the uninhibited nature of this audience and its unspoiled appetite for living, as well as the growing experience of children with sophisticated entertainment techniques in television. High standards are necessary to the staging of the themes of man's universal existence—dimensions of discovery and wonder; sagas of man against himself, opposed by his worser nature or even by nature itself in disasters, numbers, ignorance, or agony; the enthusiasms of man, his avid pursuit of half-perceived possibilities for new worlds, unrealized liberties, audacious actions. Despite the cult of pessimism and angry arguments about values in

---

*   Officials of Disney World in Florida have accumulated statistics that suggest the past is more novel than the future now, based on preference for attractions of yesterday compared with Tomorrow Land.

drama, the most dynamic theatre of this century has been written by poets who nurtured faith in man despite the evidence of the times. This is implicit in the works of Eliot and de Montherlant no more than in the writing of Shaw and Brecht. Production must not betray these dramatists with shoddiness, nor must it fail their faith by performance that gives the lie to the truth of a poet.

Theatre for children must be concerned with making visible the tales and images of our deepest fears and conflicts, our highest hopes and aspirations. These legendary revelations are "myths" because they are truer than facts, older than history, larger than knowledge. They are embodiments of the world's wisdom, visions of the race. These recurrent and apparently self-generative dreams, for all peoples know them, are links between an otherwise lost past and an unimaginable future. They define our possibilities and prove our endurance. They are our great song against loneliness and our ultimate defense against madness.

I welcome and cherish the opportunity to make this kind of theatre, a theatre that may chill, mystify, clarify, and, rarely but wonderfully, purify. It provides treasured reason to create communion through the ritual of the myth. I regard the making of rituals as the central act of theatre. They are the public crystalization of actions that privately stimulate and fortify us. They may publicly unveil and celebrate our private motives and objectives. Everything that occurs—words, gestures, symbols, music—is consonant with our perceptions of things as they are. At the climax something fundamental happens. A tyranny is destroyed, a faith is vindicated, justice is done, a marriage is made, a man becomes king. Each, alone, hesitant, inarticulate, mortal, grows and matures through rituals. This is the very essence of man's childhood sense. I want theatre for the descendants of our race to be just such a celebration, an event of affirmation, strengthening and renewing. The end of the matter is, in Mark van Doren's phrase, "not so much to tell a story as to fix a vision."

Most of the better plays in the world repertoire for children are adaptations, and the best of them tend to be adaptations of folklore and legends enshrined in beloved literary works. The homework is extensive. I always find my way back to original sources, seeking the occasion that led to the work in the beginning. Then I work forward through the numerous incarnations and shapes into which artists have cast the material. The comment of literary or music critics casts further light on the original. Beyond novels, poems and plays, some of these stories metamorphose into opera, ballet, paintings, sculpture. The director must immerse himself in all, observing and learning from each accretion of artistry. It was Lewis Carroll who wrote, "How do I know what I mean until I see what I say?" Precisely. There is the ultimate goal of theatre, seeing what we say.

A few years ago I chose Molière's *The Miser* and followed that decision with a long plunge into his major works and a new look at his life. The Ramon Fernandez biography of Molière was then new and proved a boon. I read widely of his company and theatre, consulting teachers of French and the French Information Agency. Noted contemporary French producers of Molière, especially Jean Villar and Jean-Louis Barrault, have written extensively of their views and approaches to his comedy. Only then did I determine to follow four specific directions: history of seventeenth-century France; the music and paintings of that period; the *commedia dell'arte*, so influential on Molière's craft; and the literary sources of *The Miser*. It was as though I had launched ships to the points of the compass. Eventually, after long voyages, each brought me around the world to Molière.

Of all the "cargo" accumulated on those journeys, I will share but one item. *The Miser* is Molière's least original play. He borrowed it from Plautus, who had lifted it from the Greeks two centuries before Christ. Luckily for me, I had staged the Plautus comedy as a musical in graduate school, and its contrivances are part of my own experience. Molière took this character, an old curmudgeon consumed with avarice, endowed it with devices of the Italian comedy, and set it in seventeenth-century France. An Americanized variant of the character was widely performed for the last fifty of Jack Benny's thirty-nine years. The Molière piece is unlimited caricature. Its episodes are platitudes that Molière transformed into axioms. Old Harpagon is inhuman, "a sort of beast fable," as Fernandez puts it. He is real but preposterous, a madman blind and deaf in his folly, severed from family and mankind, flailing at the world and hilariously striking himself each time. Of course he is dangerous, but the comedy arises from the fact that society outwits him and he is his own victim. Harpagon is incapable of change. Events merely illuminate his psychology. Molière did not believe that experience alters fools.

I chose to accentuate the miser's obsession. Every device of greed was explored—keys, locks, chains, traps, chests, stealth, stalking, spying, red herrings, suspicion. The methods of the *commedia* were experimented with and widely employed—pratfalls, double and triple takes, exaggerated blows, makeup styled like masks. The characters were associated with their Italian originals, vastly enriching Molière's scanty suggestions for his stereotypes. The actors were enveloped in the music and painting of the period for six intensive weeks of rehearsal. The conclusion was a ritual-in-extremis of the lunatic fallacy that possessions create happiness, executed with the precision of a farce-ballet. The setting was a vision of sunlight and flowers, a transparent interior of ostrich-plume fleur-de-lis. Beyond one could survey the garden where Harpagon buried his cash box and transplanted heart beneath the golden crowns. A net of translucent, enlarged spring flowers floated above the antic household, peacefully exuding love and beauty lost only to the monied-mentality of the distraught miser. Adults loved the play like children, while children responded with spontaneous joy, shrieking at the miser's frustrations and self-deceit, yet touched by his delusions.

A year later came *Reynard the Fox.*

Because my wife was commissioned to design costumes and makeup for the book of the play, published by the Anchorage Press, we had well over a year for preparations.

My personal fox chase was facilitated by Donald Sands' then new book, *The History of Reynard the Fox.* Reynard is a folk hero, whelped into literature by monastic scholarship in Flanders. Two other Flemish poets burnished his exploits before he dashed away to fame. So great is his vitality that he managed to survive the deadly embrace of academic approbation and the lethal sanction of respectability imparted by Fontaine, the Brothers Grimm and Goethe, no less. Despite the applause of kings and poets, Reynard never lost his wily ways and winsome foxiness.

It is strange that this extraordinary creature became the hero of the little man, for his loyalties are of the blood, like a true aristocrat. Of course his first and last impulse is survival in a world of many larger beasts. He is human enough to have a streak of meanness, but he is too clever to be predictable, and he has a devastating flair for fake humility. Like most of us he acts on impulse and reflects at leisure. Everyone secretly admires him, and almost everybody hesitates to admit it. The man who put Reynard into English in 1481, the printer William Caxton, was moved to postscript this disclaimer: "If anything be said or written herein that may grieve or displease any man, blame me not, but the fox, for they be his words and not mine."

Behind Reynard is a living myth that links us all, our ancient kinship with animals, and our love-fear relationship with the creatures who supply so many comforts and necessities for us, often at their dear expense. Moralists have often mused about the beast in man, and every man has laughed at the man in beast. Solomon sent the sluggard to learn from the ant. George Orwell made stinging political satire in his *Animal Farm.* Generations have laughed at Brer Rabbit, Pooh, and Snoopy. Disney had a winning way with a mouse, but Reynard may be the greatest of all.

The Arthur Fauquez adaptation captures him for the stage. This rogue-hero adds a skip to our pulse. We glimpse ourselves idealized into nimble wits and clever devils, not as desperate survivors of the world but cool, debonair, superior to all peril. Life may be a grim adventure, but it may also be a lark. Tricky as the chase may be, a prank will sweeten the day. This smirking rascal in shocking orange is irresistible. A glimpse of his white-tipped tail arrogantly bouncing over a meadow is a call to romance.

Our production made satire of throne and church and the time-serving barons who, for all their airs and titles, were only bears and wolves. The actors went to the zoo for protracted analysis. They came back alive with mannerisms and rhythms basic to the ritual of Reynard. No less important, they returned with great respect for the integrity of these animals. There was to be no ridicule or cheap humor at the expense of creatures merely because they walk on four feet or wear a different mask. Nor would we try to inject human mannerisms into porcupines and bears. The designer caught the animal essence in fabric and paint. I pursued it in mime and business. And in all of it we found the minds of animals and the spirit of their lives. It is no exaggeration to note that the applause has never ceased, not that it is simply for what we did but because of the myth we celebrated so infectiously and truthfully. Audiences discovered themselves in the production and applauded in recognition.

That is enough retrospection about plays I have produced that are fundamentally addressed to all humankind, or, if you will, to children. There have been many others: *Macbeth* (a natural for children, with its witches and murders, its intrigue, its poetry-in-twilight, and the titanic struggle against evil ambition); Sophocles' *Electra; Don Quixote; A Midsummer Night's Dream, The Tempest, The Winter's Tale, The Merry Wives of Windsor, Romeo and Juliet, Henry V; The Great Cross-Country Race.* Notice there is not a plastic title among them. Each is authentic theatre rooted in the widest experience of mankind. Would you be startled if I tell you I regard *The Book of Job* as theatre for children? Across a decade I have observed families in the summer performances of this play in Kentucky, and I assure you that children ages five to twelve are often more completely involved and receptive to the mystery, the ritual, the atmosphere of man's eternal questions than their parents. Adults intellectualize the experience of *Job*, observing shadows or chant, or get lost in words and feel cut off because they don't understand a phrase. Children accept the event in all its ceremony and magic, absorbing the ambiance, thrilling to spectacle. More, they often intuit the agony of Job more perceptively than their parents. They have not been cautioned that poetry is "difficult" or taught that the Bible is incomprehensible, unless schooled by specialists. All of these works are susceptible to my two key questions: What is within you? And where am I in you?

A little gratuitous advice. I feel many of my directorial colleagues oscillate between stereotype solutions or willful experimentation. I shudder when I think of belaboring the obvious, but I grow queasy when I think of what is often done in the name of experiment. Improbable stunts imposed on a play, such as mom's hat on the family poodle, or stripes on a white rooster, merely call attention to themselves. Stereotypes result from second hand knowledge and making do with leftover impressions of other people's work.

There are endless ways to the relevant and remarkable. I believe we often fail to be imaginative because our grasp is small. We charge off after one impression, determined to serve it even if we wreck the stage. Ideas must be tested repeatedly against the total play. Keep searching. Analyze all the implications. Never ignore a dimension of a play or character because you prefer another. I think one must sift a play again and again and again, especially after you think you've found it all. Do it again. Let the dust settle. Don't do all your analysis in a single period, even if it is a month long. Go away and return unexpectedly. The shape of a surprise may emerge. It is widely taught in play-directing courses that a play may be distilled to a single, central idea. This is a widely held theory, but it is not true. Only a dull play or character is strung with one string. Great plays are always more than a single theme or concept. It would be wicked to reduce *Hamlet* or *Quixote* to a solitary idea. Our task is to reveal all we can see. Theatre exists to waken a world awareness. Pursue every image through art history, through psychology, into poetry and religion. I believe each possibility we glimpse may be made visible, may contribute to the texture of performance even if it is by nature in low relief. Seek the boldest expression consistent with the significance of the myth you are wrestling with. Prolong the homework. Never rush into production. Make the time to enlarge your quest to include the curiosity and imagination of others. No one has a monopoly on insight and invention. Never commence rehearsals with a preserved trophy of your research, curious and evocative but dead. Part of the art of directing is the timing of others' involvement in the creative act. Remember, the ultimate tests of our work as directors are not "experimentation" nor even "invention." The tests are "appropriateness" and "vitality." Banish "experimentation" and "invention" to the vocabulary of critics.

I have one more word of advice. Style. But I cannot reach it without returning to my earlier caution against clichés. Too often the theatre we make for young people is arrived at by a willful suspension of our experience as theatre people. Malpractice and bromides are indulgences that we would never inflict on an adult audience. Gamesies and low cabaret humor (pleasant enough if brilliantly performed in a night club) on the level of bouncing bottoms and boisterous bosoms, of two-liners, of booze and personalities is an ancient form of theatrical entertainment that needs no defense and deserves no condemnation. But its employment—its technique, that is—is widespread in theatre for children. Many of the professional children's theatres are the worst offenders. My complaint is not moral. Children are realists. My charge is waste—waste of the audience, for they are so much more alive than such mindless and artless clichés. They deserve infinitely more. Yet we often inflict devices and performances on children that even cabaret would professionally blush before doing. I am referring to such perverse and persistent children's theatre practice as:

(a)   Disney clichés about wide-eyed and innocent bears and wolves.
(b)   Unsupported, shrill voices of unrelieved decibels.
(c)   The custom of actors jumping into one another's arms when startled.
(d)   Rump-bumping preliminary to discovering another person.
(e)   The creature that usually introduces the play.
(f)   Undigested gimmicks such as strobe lights with or without pretext (I cannot imagine a pretext) or direct address to the audience regardless of script style.
(g)   Eye-blinking, O-mouths.
(h)   Fake-fake voices.
(i)   Age portrayed as back-clutching, frenetic hobbling by imbeciles.
(j)   Physical touching and torso handling of one's partner regardless of characterizations or situation; no one ever converses without holding onto somebody.
(k)   Goosing the actors.
(l)   Collective trembling.
(m)   An incredible tolerance for salivating affection.

Dan Sullivan of the *The New York Times* made the definitive statement about these things recently in words I would write on the forehead of every director who would stage plays for children: "May I suggest we save "camp" for the grown-ups, and for the children substitute Quality? Maybe even Art?"

Style

All work in the theatre rests on that elusive and mysterious element. If universal theatre (the best name I know for so-called "children's theatre") is concerned with the focus of a life vision and the incantation of that vision into action, then the *way* or *style* of the ritual performance is central. Style is the way we make the world larger than our petty personal concerns and identity, waking us to a greater life both within and without. The conclusion of Hamlet's "making ready" begins with a stylistic decision and ends with stylistic mastery. This must never be compromised. Compromise is dilution of the theatre-theatrical; it reduces performance to ho-hums, a terrible attitude for the living to feel about an intensification and magnification of life.

I demand more style rehearsal of my actors than I do of the text. *How* we do the play is more important than *what* we do. "Whats" are opening doors, serving coffee or a drink, smoking a cigarette, a cry, a kiss, reading a newspaper. We all know these "whats," for they are the commonplaces of our lives. But *how* Margaret Rutherford served coffee; *how* Clark Gable opened a door; *how* W. C. Fields served a drink; *how* Marilyn Monroe kissed; *how* Julie Harris cried—these are theatrical verities, the quintessence of style.

Oh, you may be thinking, why don't you talk about plays for children? It is the plays that are my problem, not the actors or the style.

All right. You feel the fault in much of the theatre for children may be solved by playwrights and publishers? I submit that the problem is larger than scripts. The most successful plays I have staged are not essentially better plays than many others in any literary or theatrical sense. They happen to be plays that my actors, my wife as designer, myself as director have more accurately apprehended in their essence, more exactly perceived in their mythical form, and realized into an evocative and polished performance. More simply stated, we found an appropriate style and mastered it. Believe me, the world knows what is meant when it *sees* what we are saying. In an era of antistyle, such stylistic absorption becomes priceless and unique. After all, two fundamentals of the theatre are differentness and showmanship. I am going one way while almost all of my colleagues are stampeding another. I may be wrong, for the numbers are with them these days of games and feeling. I, too, love games and feeling. But I cannot believe that intuitive imaginations in untutored bodies are somehow superior to disciplines and developed imaginations in skilled bodies, bodies with trained voices, accomplished speech, and brightly literate minds. I do not believe that argot is an equivalent of a wide vocabulary and that sensation has supplanted intelligence. Sometimes I pause, uncertain, looking after my colleagues. But I can't see them because of the crowds at my shows.

My friends, our work lives or dies in our productions. The script is but one element. We want it to be the best. It rarely is a masterpiece. Even the best plays ever written have been repeatedly, even reverently massacred on the stage. Don't allow the script to be a scapegoat for our other failures. The equation is not complete until we have taken the play we chose, with the people, budget, space and time we have, and made our best theatre with them as we are at this moment. The moment of truth is nothing less than full-blooded, emotionally rousing, sensually overwhelming, adrenalin-draining theatre! Not the playwriting but theatre. The literary act is an art in itself. So is our theatre-making.

I have heard that there are about three thousand producers of plays for children in America. Three thousand "songbirds" swinging on the high-tension wires of our times, everyone of us singing a lovely song of our theories and theatre. But tell me now, in the isolation of your head and the silence of your heart, how many of these three thousand songbirds of us *really* can use our wings? Is the fault in the writing? Is the fault in our flying?

The Paper Bag Players in *Everybody, Everybody*.

Judith Martin, founder and producer of The Paper Bag Players, was born in Newark, New Jersey, and studied drama at the Neighborhood Playhouse in New York and dance with Martha Graham. She subsequently performed with Merce Cunningham's group and taught creative drama and movement to children. In 1958 she formed The Paper Bag Players, a professional company that has developed an original format of dance, dialogue, and song based on children's ideas and experiences.

The Paper Bag Players has achieved national and international recognition for its revolutionary approach to children's theatre and its consistently high standard of work. Paper bags, cardboard cartons, and ordinary household articles are used imaginatively for mounting.

During the nearly twenty years of the company's existence the "Bags" has performed for close to a million children in nineteen states and has made eight tours overseas. It has won such top awards as the 1971 American Theatre Association Jennie Heiden Award, the 1972 Obie (Off Broadway) for raising the level of children's theatre, the New York State Award for "lasting contribution to the artistic form of children's theatre," and the New York City Bicentennial Certificate. Because the actors work as an ensemble, their productions reflect the creative efforts of the company rather than ideas of a single person. Their point of view and methods of working are described by Judith Liss, administrator, and Nancy Lloyd, company member.

9   THE PAPER BAG PLAYERS*

JUDITH LISS AND
NANCY LLOYD

*J*udith Martin writes, designs and directs the shows for The Paper Bag Players. Donald Ashwander composes the music. This company produces original plays for children in a unique style that has brought it international recognition as an innovator in children's theatre. Judith Martin collaborating with Donald Ashwander, sketching ideas with leading actor, Irving Burton, and using the entire cast in rehearsal, develops theatre pieces that integrate story, music, dance, and a dramatic use of paper props.

It is difficult to separate the various elements that make up the Paper Bag theatre, but for purposes of description we will try to discuss each element separately. To begin with the subject matter, Judith Martin's ideas deal with events and experiences that confront children and adults in a contemporary society. Her stories are modern-day allegories. She chooses both puzzling and commonplace situations taking an unexpected, unpredictable point of view. While most of her short plays are humorous, many are lyric and all are fanciful. A bar of soap tries to persuade a little boy to take a bath; a girl milks a cardboard cow and out comes a carton of milk; a street cleaner falls in love with his trash; a pair of lips escape from a lipstick ad; an old woman is lost in a snowstorm; a family is diverted from their summer vacation by a fruitless search for their dream hamburger. The stories are told in short cartoonlike scenes. Some are acted out, some are

* This article is based on interviews with Judith Martin, Donald Ashwander, and Irving Burton. The material was collected and edited by Judith Liss and Nancy Lloyd.

danced, some are sung, and some are developed by the actors' painting on
the stage.

The Paper Bag Players is not only a theatre of allegories, it is very much
a musical theatre. This musicality comes from the force of composer Donald Ashwander. His songs, score, and musical ideas are an essential and
basic part of all the Paper Bag plays. He is so much part of the production
that his presence on the stage playing and performing seems natural. He
has chosen for his instrument the electric harpsichord, which when backed
by a Rhythm Master and various small instruments for sound effects has
the volume and variety of a small orchestra. He is a one-man band supplying the rhythmic drive, the lyric background, and the contemporary sound
that infuses every show. His sophisticated and complex style is thoroughly
American. One of Donald Ashwander's great talents is the ability to write
songs that one cannot get out of one's head. The titles give a hint of their
wit and fun—"Hot Feet," "Move Over," "Rocks," "I Won't Take a Bath."
The music is as catchy as the titles, and the audience leaves the theatre
humming his tunes.

In the tradition of musical theatre the actor must be a unique personality
as well as an accomplished performer. Irving Burton, the company's leading actor, is a great far- out comic. Unusual, eccentric, surprising, and always convincing, his dynamic style fuses movement, acting, and singing.
His ability to throw himself into far-fetched and fanciful situations is often
responsible for making a story believable. If he had not done it, no one
would believe that an ice-cream cone could be romantic; that a bathtub
could be self-righteous; that an uncouth glutton could be poignant and
lovable. He is the main-stay of the acting style of The Paper Bag Players.

Paper and cardboard, paints and crayons are of course basic elements in
The Paper Bag Players' theatre. The props and scenery designed by Judith
Martin function in several ways—sometimes as a caricature of the image
and sometimes as an abstraction. For example, a jagged piece of cardboard
gives the impression of an alligator, a refrigerator box represents a
crowded tenement. It is not the prop itself, but the movement of the prop
by the actor that creates the illusion. Costumes or props are drawn, even
constructed, by the actors on stage as part of the action. Sometimes loose
amounts of paper that cannot be completely controlled are used deliberately. There is the feeling that the paper is alive. A dance skit, "Little
Litter," uses the feeling of "live" paper. It is a fantasy about a street cleaner
and his world of trash. Two well-dressed pedestrians calmly unravel a roll
of wax paper, tear a piece off, drop it, unravel more, tear off more. A
conscientious street cleaner tries to clean up, but the wax papepr is unrav-
eled too fast for him. Eventually he is enveloped in the paper. The combination of the littering pedestrians, the bewildered street cleaner, the un-

predictable and overwhelming amount of wax paper, set against Ashwander's lyrical score, add up to a powerful haunting theatre piece.

Still another skit using "live" paper is "Earthshake," a scene from *Dandelion*, a play based on evolution. "Earthshake" came about by using a huge brown paper bag left over from another show. Irving Burton put it over his head and began to dance inside it. The mass of moving paper mysteriously changing its shape and form suggested molten lava and volcanic eruption and was appropriate for a scene showing the beginning of the world. Even when movements were set, and the show performed regularly, the paper itself remained unpredictable. It always did something a little surprising. It was "alive."

"Shoes" evolved from the use of painted props. Judith Martin recalls that one evening she was working in the studio with the usual supply of cardboard boxes. With no particular purpose in mind she painted two big shoes on four-foot-long boxes and two little shoes on foot-long boxes. She found them absurd and amusing but could not place them in a story. When the company arrived the next morning to work on new material, they were drawn to the boxes. The cast danced and talked and eventually arrived at a scenario: Two couples with boxes for shoes dance together to Donald Ashwander's ragtime music. The couple with the "big shoes" bump into each other and are discontented. They flirt with the couple who are wearing the "little shoes." Partners are exchanged. Now, with better matched boxes on their feet, the couples do the most intricate and complicated dance combinations. Wearing the most unlikely props on their feet, and carried away by the music, the couples dance with agility and grace, making an absurd and comic picture.

In *Little House* the entire skit is set in a cardboard refrigerator box. *Little House* is a short musical play about four people surviving in an overcrowded city. As the scene opens, the flat side of the box faces the audience and is painted to represent a street of tiny apartment houses. The box turns around and it is the interior of a one-room apartment. Four friends live inside. The cardboard room has an ingenious series of pockets that hold a paper blanket, a cardboard pillow, a paper book, a cardboard shower, four plastic shower caps, four cardboard coats, four cardboard hats, a cardboard table, dishes made from crackers, pretzel forks, and a cardboard telephone. Everything is tiny and used with choreographic precision. In this space the four friends sleep, eat, shower, read, and exercise, keeping out of each other's way, singing happily and cheerfully the entire time. Their accommodation to the tiny house is complete. Suddenly, the landlord raises the rent. Their cheerfulness in deciding to search for an even smaller apartment with smaller rent tells the whole story of the modern person's distortion to fit the system. It sounds like a heavy sociological theme, but with cardboard props, precise choreography, and witty music the story achieves an impact hard to match on the American stage.

In the Paper Bag theatre the actor can abruptly shift from movement or speech to drawing or painting to better express the idea of the play. In *Bicycle Race* the bicycles in the race are drawn by the actors on large pieces of cardboard in view of the audience. A whistle blows to indicate the race has begun. Each actor, holds his drawn bicycle, does a pedalling motion with his feet, and runs with it as if he were racing. The audience accepts these hand-drawn cardboard bicycles and fully participates in the excitement of the race by booing, cheering, and applauding the contestants.

In *Snow,* a short play about the enormity of a snowstorm, the narrator begins to paint a paper background. At first his white brush strokes are small and sparse. As the snowstorm becomes more intense, the narrator's strokes become bold and finally frenzied. Eventually he paints everything on the stage white—the background, the actor's clothes, even the actor's beard. The excited action of the painting set against Donald Ashwander's mysterious lyric music gives an intense presentation of a snowstorm.

There is no format in the Bags approach to creating new pieces. Usually beginning with a rough idea, Judith Martin starts to work alone in the studio. Often she will work with Irving Burton to crystallize an idea in advance of its presentation to the cast. Donald Ashwander's musical ideas sometimes lead, sometimes follow the course of the action. The company members begin with the suggested dialogue and go about building the scene. Occasionally pieces develop in an orderly fashion. Dialogue-music-movement-props build one element on the other into a whole. More often the development is completely chaotic. The dialogue doesn't develop, but a costume idea shapes the action. A song will be inappropriate, and instead a dance will emerge. Slowly, in a zigzag, backtracking way, the ideas take shape into an organized theatrical piece. Eventually, the various pieces are linked together into the proper pattern for a complete revue that might best be described as a theatrical collage.

With this approach to theatre, The Paper Bag Players has been operating for nineteen years, ever since 1958 when Judith Martin joined with a group of artists to create the Bags. She remembers the early company as being an enormously stimulating collaborative effort. Shirley Kaplan, a painter, had a fresh uninhibited approach to theatre and a special ability to improvise with materials, paper, boxes, and found objects. Remy Charlip, a dancer and author/illustrator of children's books, first introduced the idea of using cardboard and paper for costumes and props. His highly disciplined visual sensitivity demanded that every scenic element read accurately to the audience. Sudie Bond, actress, set a standard of first-rate acting that the company has since tried to maintain. Betty Osgood came to the company as a well-known modern dancer. She was a serious artist who developed a comic style with the most fastidious detail. Her enormous warmth and appeal and irresistible humor made her the epitome of a Paper Bag personality. She established for the Bags the sense that every performer had to be a strong and distinctive personality. Daniel Jahn, a musician with the greatest devotion to the the company, improvised and composed the music for the first five Paper Bag productions. As the founding artists left to return to their own fields of interest, the structure of the company changed, and the creative and directorial responsibilities rested solely with Judith Martin.

About two years after the formation of the company there was an important nonacting addition to the group—Judith Liss, business manager. As a result of her efforts, the Bags are properly advertised, publicized, and funded. Her consistent drive and her empathy for the artistic goals of the company are important factors in this sturdy company's endurance. She established that salaries for the Paper Bag actor compare favorably with salaries for comparable work in off-Broadway and regional theatres. Her role cannot be underestimated in making the company a stable situation—a place where actors can stay and grow.

Working outside the established theatrical scene, The Paper Bag Players is a theatre of fantasy, clarity, humor, and exhuberance. It is satisfying to the most demanding adult theatre-goer as well as to a range of young audiences from the Royal Court Theatre in London to rural schools in Kentucky.

Set for *The Little Golden Key* adapted by Alexei Tolstoy. Directed by Natalya Sats for the Central Children's Theatre, Moscow.

Natalya Sats, theatrical producer, writer and musicologist, is internationally known as the founder of Children's Theatre in Russia in 1918. She established and was director of the Central Children's Theatre in Moscow in 1930; she was director of the Theatre for Young Spectators in Kazakhstow from 1945 to 1950; and she has headed the Moscow State Musical Theatre for Children since 1965. She has always based her work on the belief that children's theatre must be of the same high quality as that produced for adults.

To this end she assembled a company of professional actors and singers who perform music by the finest composers. A ballet troupe, trained at the Bolshoi School of Choreography, and a staff of artists and writers complete her staff. She and her company have traveled and performed in many cities inside and outside the Soviet Union. In 1973 she was the keynote speaker at the annual convention of the Children's Theatre Association of America held in New York City.

Natalia Sats has received a number of top state awards, including honored titles, among which are Honored Artist of the Russian Socialist Federated Republic (R.S.F.S.R.); People's Artist of the R.S.F.S.R.; State Laureate of the U.S.S.R. for Cultural Work.

10

MY VOCATION[1]

NATALYA SATS
Translated by Miriam Morton[2]

*T*he education of a director[3] begins with the study of humankind. The human being, it is often said, always was and always will be the most baffling creature to his fellow men.

Indeed, the human being is the most curious phenomenon, especially for the person who hopes to become a theatrical director. Perhaps you will say not only for this profession, and you will name a number of other specializations in which no one can excel without a creative inquisitiveness about people.

I agree. I shall even remind you of one of the favorite "games" played by the great writer Turgenev. When on a train, sitting in a row with a number

1. This is a chapter from *Novelly moyei zhisni (The Stories of My Life)*, an autobiography by Natalya Sats (Moscow: "Iskusstvo" Press), 1972. It is somewhat condensed and slightly edited by the translator.
2. Miriam Morton, translator of the essays by Natalya Sats and Zenovi Korogodsky, is well known for her translations of Russian and French literature as well as for her own books. Her *Pleasures and Palaces* and *The Arts and the Soviet Child: The Aesthetic Education of Children in the U.S.S.R.* are unique contributions to the field, whereas *A Treasury of Russian Children's Literature* has already become a classic. She has received high commendation for her writing from professional organizations, and in 1973 she received a Special Citation from the Children's Theatre Association of America for interpreting Mme. Sats' lectures at its annual convention in New York City. Mrs. Morton has made numerous trips to Russia and is well acquainted with the work of Sats and Korogodsky.
3. The author discusses the work of a theatre "rezhisser"—a director-producer. In the theatre of the U.S.S.R. the two functions are combined.

of strangers, he would try to guess from their appearance and occasional words and gestures their profession, trade, style of life, expectations, biographical details. With the force and fervor of the writer, Turgenev developed in himself the ability to observe, to penetrate into the depth of human individuality, widening through his creative imagination the merely narrow frames noticeable to the average observer.

Similar "games" help the developing artist, the author-in-the-making—but especially do they help the would-be director. We know that at times the director has to help the actor project on the stage a complex, vital, believable character from merely one or two cues provided by the playwright. Could the director, then, practice his profession without a storehouse full of accumulated observations, without his skill not only to look at life but also to see it, his skill to perceive the deep and vibrantly vital, to enlarge on minute "grains of golden truth" and do so creatively, fully, and enticingly?

Perhaps you recall the little chapter "What Is a Director?" in Gorchakov's book.[4] You will remember that Gorchakov had the good fortune to sit on a bench with Stanislavsky on Gogol Boulevard one spring evening, and to the young man's question as to whether or not Konstantin Sergeevich (Stanislavsky) considered him a director, he heard the answer: "Let me test you."

Gorchakov, expecting to shine with his erudition, awaited complex questions, but Konstantin Sergeevich said, "Here we are—the two of us sitting on this bench, on a boulevard, observing life as through an open window. People are passing us and before our eyes are occurring incidents, large and small. Tell me about all that you see."

You remember how Gorchakov lost his composure and was himself dissatisfied with his response. Konstantin Sergeevich then said, "You left out much." And he went on to mention the carriage that had drawn up at the entrance to a nearby house, the woman who emerged from it evidently carrying a sick child into the house. He also had noticed the tears in the eyes of a passing woman and a series of other happenings. He further pointed out to Gorchakov that he had ignored the telling sounds that were audible around them.

A director is a person who "knows how to observe life." Train yourself to observe life: This was the first piece of advice given to the youthful director by this great teacher.

Luckily, observing—and expanding the meaning of what I saw and what I heard through my own creative imagination—was the purpose of the

4.   N. M. Gorchakov, *Rezhisserskie uroki Stanislavskovo (Stanislavsky's Lessons for a Director)* (Moscow: "Iskusstvo" Press, 1951), pp. 39–42.

most varied games and tasks given me by my father and his artist friends
even before I became aware of the existence of my childish "I." The second
circumstance that helped in my childhood and adolescence was the desire
and opportunity to try my skill as an organizer of games and primarily of
theatrical games.

"If you have an idea—act on it," my father would say when, following his
example, I tried to establish "my orchestra" of musical toys with my little
friends as performers and myself as the conductor, or when I adapted and
"staged" familiar songs and fairy tales, first with only my sister and later
with the children in the neighborhood.

The ability to fascinate others with a theatrical concept, to understand
the personalities of the participants in a production, to assert your will
despite the caprices of some, the tendency of others to quickly lose enthusiasm—how important these are for anyone who has decided to become a
director! In his own mind he has already sketched out and sees clearly the
whole production, which the other participants will have to realize. His
vision must be captivating and clear of purpose.

An involvement with theatre, with music, or with art has preceded the
professional work of many directors, but their professional talent results
nevertheless from their inherent qualities and sensitivities, enriched by a
diversity of skills that the individual has developed within himself. My hope
to become a director some day was nourished primarily by a constant
hunger to absorb the new, especially the new in art.

Too many to mention are the influences and impressions that have
helped me become a director—a person striving to realize the goals and the
images of a play, to visualize it even when before me were only sheets of
paper with the typed or printed text; a person striving to see, to hear, to
give a many-sided, integrated stage existence to what so far was only written on paper, to be excited and to excite others with the potential of the
material, to find one's "golden key" to the play's every element, to the
individuality of each role.

Heine said:

> Between theatre and reality are the orchestra, the music, the row of
> footlights. Reality, bypassing the field of sound and stepping across
> the salient footlights, reaches the stage transformed by poetry.

I don't remember whether I knew these words of Heine's, which have since
become so meaningful to me, when I first undertook to direct a children's
production.

Real life with real people is a great artistic truth, and how difficult it is of
realization on the stage, especially in so new an art as children's threatre

was at the time I first became a director. All its literature and its principles were born at the same time as the theatre itself. To look for the truth in art is not at all the same as to find it. The truth in art never exists on the surface. It has to be unearthed with the obstinacy of a goldminer; it has to be cleansed of all alluvial matter—that is, of all superficiality; and only from the purified grains can a small ingot be obtained. The theatre, unlike any other art, has the opportunity to blend many related arts—literature, acting, mime, dance, music, and graphic expression—becoming the magnet of inspiration for a great diversity of artists.

At the time of my beginnings in this profession, many directors in their search for authenticity began to incorporate film, mainly documentary, into their theatrical productions. It seemed to me that, while broadening the potential of the stage to show documentary reality, they sacrificed the artistic integrity of the dramatic concept, thus cheapening the theatre and denying its own conventions relating to the representation of reality. Nevertheless, as Heine said:

> . . . reason never plays a leading role in the creation of works of art. They emerge from somewhere in the depths of the artist's soul, and only take on life when his creative fantasy is ready to cast upon his conception its abundance of flowers, to prune with garden shears in hand all prejudice, to cut off all that is superfluous, giving what is exceptional every chance for growth.

The concept of *Negrityonok i obeziana* (*The African Boy and the Monkey*) came to me out of the blue; the story and the director's vision sprang into mind simultaneously. I think this was the first time in the theatre—not only in ours but generally—that animated cartoon film was introduced in conjunction with live dramatic action.

Animated cartoon images are close in kind to children's drawing, with its omission of unimportant details, with its utmost concentration on the dynamic representation of the essential. Animated cartoon films, I believed, would broaden the possibilities of the stage without violating the basic artistic intention, as they helped to show quickly the changing scenes of nature and the indigenous background for some of the incidents.

My views on this were largely confirmed by the production. We see a corner in a forest glade, in the shadow of overhanging, tangled tropical vines. There are birds on the wing, elephants strolling about. On a screen to the right a thicket is projected, and in this thicket our actors, playing the parts of african children, are "hiding." They are waiting for more animals to gather in the clearing. When Nagua gives the signal, the children begin to strike their percussion instruments. The frightened beasts (in the animated cartoon) panic and run. A bewildered deer hesitates. Nagua aims his arrow at the lingering deer. He misses; the animal darts into the forest. Now the panorama of the forest moves (on the screen) with Nagua in pursuit of the deer.

At the right moment the actress who played Nagua seemed to "enter" the cartoon film. But how is it this was hardly noticeable and totally unintrusive? Because the whole style of the drawings for the animation subtly blended with the stage set designed by Gerrgi Goltz and because Nagua's costume, characteristic movements, mannerisms that the player and the director decided on for the role were identical on the stage and in the animation. The shifting from the stage action to the screen was organic in this fairy tale, so full of amazing adventures.

This was my first directorial work[5] that received great (I am not afraid of this word) recognition from our own and the foreign press, from the broad public, and, most important, from the children in the audience.

This production saw its one thousandth performance on our stage (the Moscow Children's Theatre) only six years after its premiere. It was also produced, together with the animation, in the theatres of Tbilisi, Georgia, and in other Soviet cities. It was presented at the opening of the Titian Vysotsky Theatre in Warsaw, the Mila Mellanova Theatre in Prague, and the Children's Theatre of Brno. It has been staged in Switzerland and in Turkey.

How important it is for the director to meet talented kindred spirits with whom he can sense the current theatrical atmosphere and presage the "today" of tomorrow! Leonid Polovinkin had just graduated from the Moscow Conservatory with a gold medal as pianist, composer, and conductor. A young man of uncommonly wide erudition, he had also earned two university degrees in different disciplines and was an accomplished sportsman, winning awards in a variety of competitions.

I conceived *The African Boy and the Monkey* as a pantomimic dance and wholly musical production. There were only short speaking parts, and these were limited to the Kind Woman and "the person on the proscenium"—that is, the commentator.

Polovinkin liked the story and he got to work with unrestrained youthful ardor. His music grew like the tropical forest that was the setting for this tale. The composer was most intrigued by the action in the play: the first meeting of Nagua and the monkey; its capture by the hunters; the meeting

5. It was only Natalya Sats' second attempt at directing. The play was first produced in 1927 at the Moscow Children's Theatre. It has been for the past twelve years in the repertory of Natalya Sats' Musical Theatre for Children in Moscow. It is now a balletic production, but it still uses Polovinkin's original music and Goltz's stage sets.

of Nagua and the monkey in the circus. I remember how he circled with his red pencil the central episodes in the play.

He was very much taken with the personalities of the child characters. Each African child competes with his fellows in executing a dance—and here is where the composer decided to stress the different personalities of the little contestants. Bumba was a showoff; Benga was bold, too bold, rough, and hot-tempered; Oa was tiny and timid; Baiba was self-conscious, plump, and clumsy; and so on. The characterizations were further defined in Polovinkin's music by his interpretive and varied rhythms, which suggested additional touches to the director and the actor.

> The Moscow Children's Theatre is convinced that theatre for children is an eminently proper place for the musical education of the young, and that music must affect the spectator in this theatre not only with its melodiousness but with the sum of its expressiveness. This last assumption found its bright confirmation in the immense success with the children of the music for *The African Boy and the Monkey*.
>
> Polovinkin's music definitely takes into account the child's psychology but without losing the subtlety and wit characteristic of his compositions. His music for this children's play shows us what modern music must sound like to assure a full response from the modern child.[6]

Following the success of *The African Boy . . .,* the composers N. Ya. Miaskovsky and S. M. Vasilenko and the conductors N. S. Golovanov and A. V. Nezhdanova came to work in our theatre.

My first collaboration with a set designer was with the painter-architect Georgi Goltz. It was an extremely happy one. He found the basic color tonality for the play and insisted on using it to the full. *The African Boy . . .* in his mind's eye was suffused with golden-yellow tones. Africa. Sun and sand. There is a semicircular elevation on one side of the stage rising to a height of four meters and divided into three steplike levels. The players move variously on its slope, and each figure is thus more strongly focused. This hillock and everything else on the stage is immersed in a sunny-yellow color.

The first scene is in the desert, and here a single green cactus is added to the basic scenery. The second scene is in the form of animation but without the lowering of a screen. The cartoon is projected onto the yellow backdrop.

6.   In *Zhizn' iskusstra* (*The Life of Art*), issue of June 7, 1927.

To the forest scene are added tropical vegetables, palm and coconut trees, tangled vines. There are only a few of these, just enough to give the impression of a forest (the time of the scene is late in the evening).

Then finally the circus scene. Here we use the same set but with two vivid posters placed in a way to suggest a circus arena.

Goltz designed a single set that served the different scenes well and made it possible to meet easily the needs of a great variety of scenes on which an uninterrupted series of episodes evolved.

It often happened that all the tickets to *The African Boy* . . . were sold out well in advance. One day a mother and her little girl came to the box office and were told that there were no tickets left for that day. The woman tried to console her disappointed little daughter. "You've already seen this show. There are no tickets left. Let's go to the zoo. There we can see a real monkey." The little girl flared up, saying, "They don't have a real one there. The one here is real!"

The African Boy and the Monkey was intended for six- to eight-year-olds, but it was loved and seen again and again not only by the young children but by boys and girls of all ages and even by grownups.

Ours was a theatre for children. We were never embarrassed by that "for," nor could we understand those artists who openly (I cannot say "honestly") declared: "I work for the time being in children's theatre, but I couldn't care less for whom I work."

We passionately believed that since the Revolution had opened up erstwhile nonexistent cultural opportunities for the young, we were committed to use them in every way and with utmost creativity, not separating the overall demands of dramatic art from that "for" but understanding and loving the children for whom new artistic works were being created.

I like the naïve theatre for little ones. Naïveté is not foolishness. We diligently studied the requirements of children of different ages but not so as to supply them with a theatrical experience that would be easily and mindlessly received. I believe that plays for children have to be not simple but demanding—not soft as *kasha* (mush) but hard as a nut, a nut that their little teeth can crack. Yes, their own little teeth so that they can themselves crack it, grow on it—that is, understand what they have seen on the stage.

I directed-produced seventeen plays at the Moscow Children's Theatre. Some were addressed to the little ones, others to school children of the middle grades, still others to teenagers. Awareness of the "addressee" invariably helped me creatively. It seems to me that the director-producer always carries on a sort of creative dialogue with his audience-to-be as he formulates his ideas about a new production.

Which plays and what age group did I most favor? Allow me to answer that question in the words of the piano virtuoso Sviatoslav Richter: "I love most the music which I am playing today." If the director could not fall in love with every new project, he could hardly be a director.

Beginning with the directing of *The African Boy . . .*, I felt compelled to find common ground with the scenic artist, to find with him the key to an integrated image (conceptual and staged) of the projected production. We had to agree on a common theme, on the central problem. Variations essential for the proper development of the action had to remain congruous with the core theme. Integration? Coherence? Yes, theatre must be integrated and coherent; this is its essence. To bring the verities of life to the stage means being able to make use of theatrical techniques for expressiveness in the art.

Directing soon occupied first place in my thoughts and my life. Every new play was a new birth, a unique directorial creation. Having decided on a new production, I became its "fan," fell madly in love with its theme, kept up a running battle with myself until I was satisfied with the way I sensed the sharpness of its meaning, the depth and vitality of its characters, until I saw clearly the setting of the scenes and found the means for projecting the atmosphere of the forthcoming production.

To uncover the essence of the play's idea, to reveal the inner depths of the text is most basic to the director's role. But once I found the form for expressing the content—in the staging, the gestures, the dynamics of action and pause— I struggled to realize it down to the most minute details.

When the director finds what he has been striving for, it seems to me that from that moment there is no "or" for him but "only this way." There are those who are inclined to call this formalism. I do not agree. It is rather a precise awareness of what the director has sought, and, having found it, he does not want, under any circumstnces, to lose it or surrender it.

Without form the content of art never finds its ultimate power of expression. Only when every theatrical artist involved in a production focuses on his chosen form can the overall theatrical enterprise gain its greatest coherence of expressiveness.

Theatre artists value good directors, those with a gifted imagination, but they love most of all the directors who can help each of them individually to bring his role to perfection, to grow in his new part. To find the "golden key" to every artist's individuality is the director's greatest challenge. But without the willing interaction of the author, the scenic artist, the composer —of all the artists—of the electricians and others, there will be no production, and the director is the navigator who, having united all of them into a fine crew, steers the craft to new and splendid shores.

PART IV

Standards for Children's Theatre

Mary Jane Evans is professor of theatre at California State University in Northridge, California. She holds a B.S. degree from Northwestern University, where she studied with Winifred Ward, a Master's degree from Michigan State University, and has done additional study at Western Reserve University, the University of Wisconsin at Eau Claire, and the University of Minnesota. She was co-author (with Jed Davis) of the well-known college text *Children's Theatre: Play Production for the Child Audience*. Professor Evans has served on many committees of the Children's Theatre Association of America and the American Theatre Association. She was a consultant to the committee writing the Drama/Theatre Framework for the California Public Schools and is a leader of theatre activities in that region.

THEATRE FOR CHILDREN: ART FORM OR ANARCHY?

11

MARY JANE EVANS

*H*ow trite it seems to begin by commenting on the changing times in which we live! Somehow, though, it seems necessary. Without belaboring the point, we are painfully aware that we live in a complicated age where virtually every facet of life is being scrutinized, questioned, and altered. The impact of change surrounds us, influences us, often alarms us. Certainly it forces us to take a new look at the old, to change with the times, to readjust. Historically, the arts not only reflect but often become instruments of change. Theatre for children is part of the arts scene, and, as such, it has felt and reacted to the turbulence of this era.

Not too many years ago it was relatively simple to discuss theatre for children and to arrive at comfortable descriptions of the functions of all the artists involved in children's-theatre production. We had a fairly rigid and generally accepted definition that allowed us to operate from what seemed to be a stable philosophical and practical base. When the time came to do a show, the director could choose from a woefully limited selection of scripts. Some, in desperation, wrote their own. But the script was there, central to the project. The director worked from a conventionalized set of goals, moved with the company through a more or less prescribed series of rehearsal phases, and presented a production.

Although there always were some who departed from the accepted pattern, most discussions of theatre for children automatically assumed that it started with a script based on literature or, in some cases, a script created from an original story line developed by a playwright. We used to be able to assert with stolid certainty that "this is children's theatre and that is creative drama," and while they were deemed to be mutually complementary, their philosophy, goals, and techniques were, for all practical purposes, mutually exclusive. That no longer is true. Indeed, any single guiding principle for producing plays for children seems to have been abolished. Producers now refuse to pay slavish attention to traditional "do's" and "don't's" when they think of child audiences. Some of this grows out of an expanding concept

119

of what constitutes a play, a performance, and a child. Some of it is a result
of rebellion against conformity.

Certainly we still do have many productions of conventional scripts, and
the range of printed dramatic material has widened considerably. Production modes have diverged from the traditional proscenium, arena, and
thrust into a seemingly endless variety of forms and styles. We hear of and
see story theatre, improvisational theatre, instant theatre, participation
theatre, to name but a few. Although these are the broad and general
categories into which much of the "new" theatre for children falls, there
seem to be as many departures from the conventional as there are
producers.

This expansion of approach is healthy and necessary. It certainly has
shaken up the theorists. It has generated renewed interest in producing
plays for children, encouraging many who would have no part of the
traditional to try their hands at the game. This is all to the good. Without
experimentation there can be no progress. The question is, how solid is our
footing? Has experiment led to anarchy? In selecting new paths to follow,
how much that is valid is being overlooked? How much that is trite and
inherently offensive is being perpetuated and reinforced?

On the face of it, the popular new production modes are the essence of
simplicity. The script no longer is sacrosanct. Many groups work without
one. Settings and costumes designed to provoke the imagination rather
than specifically define, reliance on the actor rather than on technically
elaborate production support, bringing the audience fully into the performance—these techniques give much greater freedom to a company to
get together and make theatre with joy, honesty, and daring. Nevertheless,
there are pitfalls. Just as the "old" theatre for children had its well-inten-
tioned but uninformed producers and its exploiters, so does the "new." In
addition, too many companies believe that it takes nothing special to succeed with newer and less elaborate production modes. This is a delusion.
The less support a company has from magnificent scenery, painstakingly
designed costumes, and magical lighting, the more important become the
quality of the material, the attitude and artistry of the director and actors,
and the director's nurture and control of the end product.

No theatre ever is easy. The experimental is even less so. If it seems to
be, something is wrong. Change for its own sake cannot solve problems or
eliminate weaknesses unless those effecting change base their explorations
and efforts on solid principle and practice.

Despite the fact that through the years we espoused solid principles and
claimed to be following solid practices, playwrights and producers often
have been criticized for their simplistic approach. With considerable justifi-
cation we have been accused of undervaluing the intelligence of children.
Noise has substituted for substance; frenetic activity has taken the place of

gripping dramatic action; shrieks, pratfalls, unmotivated slapstick, chorus-line blocking, music and dance numbers that come from nowhere; frenetic chases through the audience; exploitation of emotion—all these certainly have been part of our theatre. And all of them certainly represent funda-mental and unpardonable violations of the dignity, intelligence, and sensi-bility of the the young. Producers have been accused of lacking courage to depart from the tried-and-true story to present relevant themes, to show things as they are. There is validity in these charges. In our comfortable self-righteousness many of us have insulted the intelligence of our audi-ences as we have failed to acknowledge their ability to draw conclusions and make value judgments.

It would be nice to be able to say that new forms, styles, and content in and of themselves have stripped away the pandemonium, pap, and poppy-cock. Unfortunately, it cannot be said. Since 1972 the Southern California Educational Theatre Association has held an annual Children's Theatre Festival where numerous companies assemble to present productions. Most of them have adopted the newer modes. All of them are supposed to represent the best that is going on. Most of them do, and they get positive and enthusiastic response from their audiences. On the other hand, evi-dence that advancement does not necessarily mean progress can be found in some comments gleaned from evaluation forms turned in by junior reviewers:

"I didn't believe them." (six-year-old)

"I don't like it. They weren't involved in it." (nine-year-old)

"Too many songs." (nine-, ten- and thirteen-year-olds)

"I didn't like the noise of the argument." (eight-year-old)

"There are too many questions that ask the same thing, and I'm tired of answering questions." (dictated by a five-year-old)

There also were numerous check marks in the "No" box following the question, "Did the actors listen to the answers the audience gave?"

Adult reviewers from the profession expressed their concern about flashiness substituting for substance, failure to develop intrinsically moti-vated action, costumes that looked like gleanings from the thrift shop, lack of dimensionality in characterizations, satisfaction with any performance that roused the audience to the kind of shrieking emotional frenzy usually associated with athletic contests, and repetition *ad nauseam* of pleas to the audience to shout loudly at the count of three in order to resolve the dramatic conflict. It did not happen in Los Angeles, but one reviewer told of an incident where a fourth-grader responded to one of those exhorta-tions, "It's your problem." Perhaps more children should demonstrate the same kind of courage.

One of the major goals of the festival is providing opportunities for

producing units to meet with reviewers to analyze and evaluate performances. Almost invariably the companies that were on shakiest ground
were the most resistant to comment and suggestion. For years we have
lamented the fact that children's-theatre people get together and talk a
great deal, but sometimes they are not very good listeners.

These troubling observations generate more questions. First, has anything really changed? Apparently not. Second, in our efforts to generate
overt audience involvement are we forgetting about the magic of theatre?
It seems that oftentimes we are. Theatre magic is fragile, easily destroyed,
but it need not be. It can be generated, whatever the production mode, be
it anything from a totally staged proscenium production to a two-actor
improvisation in a shopping center, park, or gymnasium. It requires only
that well-trained, properly motivated and likable actors come into contact
with an audience, the one group creating and the other sharing in the
glorious art of make-believe. This means developing companies who make
theatre for the mutual delight of themselves and their audience. They must
have something to share, someone with whom to share, and do their sharing in a careful, caring, and honest way. Whether this sharing comes
through the presentation of a fully staged scripted story with aesthetic and
physical separation of actors and audience, whether it comes through direct address to the audience, or whether it comes through audience-participation activities, this is a condition of artistic success.

Companies should be free to do any kind of production they wish to do.
The fourth wall is not a sacred structure. However, in our experimenta-
tions let us make informed judgments about what to retain and what to
leave behind, for too often we find it easier to discard what is solid and pick
up on the "gimmick," to perpetuate the old/bad in our search for the new/
better.

During the turbulent Sixties a colleague was heard to comment, "There
are certain eternal verities that must remain." Despite revolutions, every
facet of existence has its solid cornerstones, and we in the theatre for
children have ours.

First, we espouse a very real concern for our audience. If we did not,
there never would have been a theatre for children. We have said that we
care about and can contribute to children's mental, emotional, spiritual,
and intellectual growth. That is good. What is not good, as noted earlier, is
that we frequently have undervalued the abilities and sensibilities of our
youth. Too often we have made judgments from our adult vantage point,
arbitrarily deciding what is right and not right for our audiences, what they
can and cannot accept, cope with, or absorb. We have been correctly accused of being self-righteous. No director should presume to produce
theatre for children until he or she has tried to arrive at an intelligent
understanding of children: what they think, what they like, what they care

about, what moves them. We in the field have not conducted enough research into the impact of theatre on children. There is, however, a wealth of information to be had in the literature of child development, education, and psychology.

We are regularly reminded that today's children are sophisticated products of a technological age. This does not mean that the content and format of television and film production should unduly influence the theatre. It does mean, though, that because of their exposure to the mass media children do know more than those who lived in a simpler age. Oftentimes they show a remarkable intellectual grasp of ideas and events. They are aware that the world does not consist of black hats and white hats, that the pure, good, and beautiful do not always win tangible rewards. They are able to make value judgments, and they are increasingly perceptive. They know when they are being "had."

Naturally this has led producers to question the validity of much scripted material that is available to them. Questioning their "relevance," many companies have rejected the classics out of hand. Others devise "modern" versions that sometimes work but more often prove to be merely bewildering. When preoccupation with relevance leads to making aesthetic decisions almost totally on the basis of here-and-now concerns, those decisions often are as ill-advised as were those for which directors of earlier times were criticized.

Relevance in itself is not bad. What is bad is focusing solely on the present and ignoring the unassailable fact that certain concerns are universally and timelessly relevant. Human personalities, instincts, fears, needs, desires, emotions do not change in fundamental ways, though our manner of dealing with them may. Here-and-now concerns certainly are important and should be dealt with, but the ephemeral nature of many of them should be acknowledged. Further, the way in which we deal with them theatrically should be carefully scrutinized. Finally, in recognizing that certain human concerns are timeless and universal, we also must remember that the good folk of the past had good and lasting ways of presenting and resolving them and that these treatments also are relevant.

Please do not read this as a reactionary plea to ignore currency, to stick solely to the tried and true. It is merely a reminder that all literature, even that whose origins are lost in time, was once current. It has remained a part of our heritage simply because it touches the core of our humanity. No one now can predict how lasting present-day treatment of contemporary topics will be. Nonetheless, those who choose to deal with them can learn from the past. No matter how timely the event, its artistic treatment will have value only if its focus is on some universal truth.

Thoughts about the child audience and the dramatic material we prepare for them remind us of another element that should not be overlooked. Many parents regularly attend productions with their children. All across the country adult organizations retain companies to present plays for children. As we who produce those plays become more open in our point of view, acknowledging and adjusting to the increasing sophistication of our primary audience, we do not always find parents and sponsors sharing our attitude. Too many of us have found ourselves criticized or refused bookings when we have presented provocative theatre that appeals to the mind as well as the imagination. How often have we heard, "It was a fine production, but it was *not* for children." This is a very real problem. Adults who pay little or no attention to the slaughter and mayhem their children view on television and, at the other extreme, adults who continue to believe that children should be sheltered from all reality are equally vocal. They protest with loud and mighty voices because they find no clear and simple moral statement in many of the newer plays or because a drama allows—nay, requires—the child to draw his own conclusions. Evil fairies, giants, Reynard the Fox, even poor old Punch are regarded as too violent for young souls to bear. In the past we have been accused of condescending to children. We must now decide whether it is better to be criticized for making young people stretch than it is to continue to be guilty of condescension. We must, however, thoughtfully determine where the boundaries are and deal with our subject matter in artistically valid performances.

New forms, styles, and content place increasing responsibility for valid artistry on children's-theatre directors. We have long said that we who direct must be theatre artists who know about, understand, respect, and like children; that we must have a firm belief that theatre for children is an important and respectable art form; that we must have respect for our integrity as artists; that we must be endowed with creative vision. Further— and sometimes we have forgotten this—we must also function as teachers. This does not mean pedantry, didacticism, or dictation but rather using to the utmost our ability to communicate with actors, bringing out what is best in them and helping them develop as human beings, assisting them in sharpening their skills, instilling a sense of discipline, purpose, and control that leads to fine ensemble work. Directors always have been asked to possess a refined sense of the fitness of things and to insist on a high standard of good taste in production. These requirements do not change.

In approaching productions that begin without a script or with a script that allows considerable latitude to the company, directors need skills that far transcend those associated with preparing a traditional theatre piece. Creating a show from scratch is no mean challenge. Working with a script that calls for direct and physical audience involvement is equally formidable.

Unquestionably, directors who are competent in creative drama always have had an advantage, but skill in leading improvised drama now is requisite to success. Not only that, actors are more and more required to master the techniques of creative drama leadership, and frequently it is the director who must provide instruction. He or she certainly must guide and shape actor preparation for audience involvement. Thus the rehearsal process becomes a training period requiring considerably more than role and ensemble preparation. When there is no script, it becomes a period of exploration. In any case, no matter how democratic and actor-centered the rehearsal process is, the director never relinquishes responsibility for the final product.

Too many performances that start from improvisation are shallow and without substance, exhibiting all the negative values that have brought criticism to traditional theatre for children but without even the saving grace of a coherent story line. Too much participation theatre is apparently aimless, unfocused, without point. In both cases it seems as if no one took charge of shaping and refining the performance. Even at festivals and showcases, such productions are defended as experimental works in progress. Is this fair to the audience? Is it theatre magic? Someone at some point has to say that the performance is ready, and until that time it should not be brought to the public.

All directors must have a sense of what they wish to achieve with every theatre piece for which they take responsibility. This requires us to put our imaginations to work. We cannot come in like a blank slate, but rather we must have a rich store of ideas and challenges to present. Improvisations have to start from stimuli that inspire and ultimately provide focus. Directors must be able to distinguish between artistic freedom and license, to give purpose and coherence to the company's work, and to see to it that goals are set. We must know when to step aside and let things happen and when to intervene. We must insist that all action be dramatic, stemming from character motivation, not from actor whim. We must require that all characterizations be credible. Nothing can be played for cheap effect. And again, the performance must be set.

While it truly can be said that any production grows and refines itself through a series of performances, the time for frank experimentation is before the opening and between, not during, encounters with the audience. No company can afford to lose sight of its obligation to share the best, most polished results of its experiments. If there is pre-show activity in the playing area, let it be staged as carefully as any scene organic to the play. If settings and properties are to be moved in view of the audience, that activity also must be staged. If there is participation, actors must be fully prepared for their interactions with the audience. If we are attempting instant theatre, actors must be carefully trained to solicit, receive, and respond to audience suggestions. We must always bear in mind the special nature of the theatre event.

These responsibilities are shared equally by directors and actors. Initially, however, it is the director who sets the tone. While casting is crucial to all theatre, and the general characteristics we seek in actors are common to all forms, special consideration must be given to selecting and training companies who will work in nontraditional modes. Here we usually are not seeking one actor for one role but versatile, spontaneous performers who are able to shift quickly from role to role. Every actor may be called on to become a narrator, an intermediary with the audience, numerous characters ranging from human to animal to fantasy, inanimate objects—anything the imagination demands. This requires great physical and mental agility, flexibility, control, and superb discipline; congeniality and willingness and ability to participate in a continuing creative process, interacting imaginatively and cooperatively with other actors, the director, and, ultimately, with the audience.

Actors must genuinely like children, respect them, and feel responsible for the nature of their interactions with them. They should be willing and able to develop and accept ethical and aesthetic standards that will define the limits of their own self-expression. Exuberance is fine and necessary, but it must be tempered by an understanding of the delicate and unique relationship that exists between adult actors and children in the audience. This is particularly true in any kind of participation theatre, where audience management is as much a part of performance as is role presentation.

All this takes time. The director has to be realistic about the length of time required to create and shape a performance. While it is reasonable to assume that a standard scripted production can be brought to performance standard in approximately four weeks of systematic rehearsal, that is not a safe assumption when an improvisational approach is followed. There will be dry periods when nothing seems to go right, and this is natural to the creative process. Time must be allowed to cross the desert. Time also is important in preparing for participation theatre, since the company not only has to be rehearsed in roles but also trained to deal directly with children, not only as a group but as individuals.

This latter training is crucial. In no other form of theatre is it so important to be sensitive to individuals and their differences. Some children want to participate and will make their desires clear—sometimes too clear. Others who want desperately to get into the act are not aggressive enough to capture attention unless actors are extremely sensitive to subtle signs. Still others want to remain aloof, to be spectators, and their wishes should be respected. No form of audience involvement should be attempted unless the performers accept their double role as actors in a theatre piece and as adults responsible for the well-being of children.

Concern with the elaborate processes of preparing actors for performance should not cause producers to overlook or minimize the importance of visual elements in nontraditional presentations. Stripped of costumes that define individual characters, what should actors wear? Are blue jeans and polo shirts or any old thing from the wardrobe enough? Not really. Despite their desire to establish intimacy with the audience, it is doubtful that actors like to be regarded as "just plain folks," and it is equally doubtful that children want them to be. They want them to be special. Thus members of the company should be dressed as if they cared. Something must set them apart from the mundane world of the playground. It is an offense to an audience that has prepared itself for a special occasion to find those responsible for it looking as if they had just come in off the street. We all should bear in mind the reaction of an eight-year-old boy who, on being taken to see one of the better-known professional improvisational companies, had but a single comment to make: "Well," he said with a shrug, "I suppose they can't afford costumes."

The same holds true of the environment we create in our theatre spaces. We are delighted that the liberated theatre for children is no longer confined to traditional theatre areas. We now know that good performances can be presented anywhere, thus broadening opportunities for increasing numbers of children to experience theatre. At the same time, liberation leads to new responsibility. The burden on the producer and the company really increases. All the requirements of sincerity and honesty in performance are intensified. Every visual element is subject to close scrutiny, and the fewer the visual elements, the more obvious each one becomes. Safety pins, Scotch tape and construction paper will be exposed for what they are. Basted seams can destroy the credibility of a king, no matter how fine his performance.

Let us think again of today's children as products of a technological age. When color television was in its infancy, we in the theatre were delighted to hear child audiences respond to an opening curtain with gasps of "Oh, it's in color!" Those days are long gone. Regardless of program content, television production values are uniformly high. Obviously the theatre cannot compete with the studio. We must bear in mind, however, that our audiences daily partake of visual feasts as they sit in front of the small screen. The presence of the living actor is not in itself sufficiently exciting to compensate for shoddy visual elements.

No matter where a discussion of theatre for children begins, it inevitably seems to end with an examination of standards. The rebels and nonconformists with venturesome daring have challenged the old ways and have freed us from the shackles of traditionalism. Unfortunately rebellion has become self-indulgence for all too many producers. In those cases, the flaws of the past do not get mended. Indeed, they become more glaring than ever. For the thoughtful, however, revolutionary surges lead to reappraisal, and the thoughtful ones among us can reach only one conclusion: Forms may change, but substance does not. The fundamental guiding principles that have been with us from the beginning do not disappear.

From *Winnie-the-Pooh* production of the Nashville Children's Theatre directed by Thomas C. Kartak.

Thomas C. Kartak is director of the Nashville Children's Theatre, one of the outstanding theatres for children in the United States. His background includes a bachelor's degree from the University of Washington, a Master of Fine Arts degree from the University of Hawaii, and a doctorate from Northwestern University. He has taught and directed on both high school and college levels and in 1972 founded the Nashville Theatre Academy in Nashville, Tennessee, the home of one of the few theatres built exclusively for children in the United States.

Mr. Kartak is also a playwright whose *Dead End Doin's* was presented at Opryland, USA. His four versions of Shakespearean plays for child audiences have been staged in Japan and Australia as well as in the United States. Thomas Kartak holds the distinction of having presented in 1976 the first play for children in the Eisenhower Theatre at the Kennedy Center.

THE SUITABILITY OF DRAMA FOR CHILDREN

12

THOMAS C. KARTAK

*T*o indulge in and appreciate the dramatic is natural to mankind. This is so for peoples of all nations and cultures, for both young and old, and for peoples of all times. Formal indulgence of this dramatic instinct may be prohibited or discouraged by a particular society, but it is nevertheless there. This being the case, there is certainly nothing foreign to human nature in introducing children to formal dramatic experience.

Children naturally seek the dramatic and enjoy indulging in it. Since drama incorporates action, and action is a necessary state of being for the growing child, the appeal of drama to the young is a dynamic appeal. It therefore becomes highly advantageous to provide the child with the dramatic experience.

There are many types of dramatic experience in which a child may indulge. While all of these may have great individual validity, this argument is concerned with only one: causing the child to witness the live presentation of a dramatic work. More specifically, we are concerned with a presentation to which the child usually comes and one prepared for him in a professional manner by an adult or group of adults.

THE SUITABILITY OF LIVE DRAMA FOR THE YOUNG

The value of causing the child to witness a theatrical presentation will be discussed presently. First, however, let us examine the value of the live-theatre experience as opposed to the mechanically presented theatre experience, be it radio, television, or motion pictures. In terms of subject matter, there need be no difference between the live and recorded theatre experience. One can be as worthwhile, as well prepared, as artistic, or, conversely, as worthless, as poorly prepared, as inartistic as the other. In terms of treatment—that is, the manner, method, and devices employed to convey the subject matter—advantages can be found for any medium of presentation, just as disadvantages are imposed by each separate medium. While I do not argue against the values of dramatic material presented on any mechanical medium, I should like to argue for the live presentation of dramatic material.

Just as the dramatic instinct is universal, so are the instincts for ritual and mystery. Although manifested in a multitude of ways, the needs for ritual and mystery are experienced by all, and satisfying those needs is therapeutic in all cases.

While drama presented on radio, television, or film can and does address the needs of ritual and mystery, live theatre has the advantage in meeting those needs with heightened impact. One feels more greatly soothed by being administered to in the areas of health and religion, for instance, on an immediate basis. As an example, a visit with one's doctor is more gratifying than a telephone call. Likewise, attendance at a Sunday church service is usually more satisfying than listening to such a service on the radio or viewing that same service as a television broadcast. In the area of the arts, a musical work has more impact when heard in concert than the same work performed by the same musicians heard recorded; an original painting viewed in a gallery is more fulfilling than a reprint viewed in a book; one's enjoyment of a ballet is heightened when the dance is viewed live.

Witnessing live actors perform the ritual of enacting a set of experiences can move an audience more deeply and more lastingly than witnessing those same actors removed from one's presence, and removed from immediacy, by the act of being presented mechanically. This is so, in part, because by performing the act of joining a live and immediate ritual, if only as a spectator, one becomes a part of that ritual, able to influence it.

As to mystery, the act of turning on a radio, television set, or motion-picture projector cannot compare in impact to the moment when the house lights dim, the curtain rises, and the stage lights come up to reveal a live actor in one's presence. Of course, there is great mystery in the workings of a radio, television set, or motion-picture projector, but that mystery does not occur to us as often nor as powerfully, since modern man generally takes these miracles for granted. Moroever, when one witnesses a mechanically reproduced drama, one may not know the outcome, but one can rest assured that it will come out. At a live theatre presentation one witnesses the audacious act of a group of people *attempting* to achieve. It is never certain that they will succeed in their attempt, and therein lies the mystery.

Live theatre, in most cases, has the additional advantage of having to appeal only to a limited and predictable audience. On the subject with which we are specifically concerned, the children's theatre of an area has the luxury of needing to appeal only to the needs and tastes of the children of that area. For example, as a children's-theatre director in Hawaii, I chose to present a play about the first Japanese to visit that island chain, and another play was presented in the style of Peking opera. These plays were given to an audience that was consistently predominantly Oriental. In Tennessee I chose to present a play about the Bell Witch, the most exciting and well-known local legendary personage. No mass-media presentations can cater so consistently to such local tastes, interests, and needs.

Finally, in viewing live theatre the specific focus of attention is left to the viewer. Devoid of such devices as close-ups, peripheral lens focus, and instant cutaway, live theatre must present a consistently fuller scene, allowing and demanding that the viewer be responsible, in part at least, for focus. This allows, again at least in part, the viewer to discover what it is he wants to discover in a scene and take away from a live theatre experience, to some extent, what he has chosen to register and take away.

Even from this brief discussion it becomes evident that the live theatre experience has something special for the child. As we shall see, that something can be of great significance.

THE SIGNIFICANCE OF LIVE THEATRE PERFORMANCES FOR THE YOUNG

A group performing for the young must have as its major function the production of the best possible live theatre presented specifically for the children who make up its audience. To define "best possible," one might use the criteria that the production be understandable and amusing to the child viewing it, yet that beyond this, the script used must have literary merit and the production of that script have artistic merit to the point that anyone viewing the production will have grown as a result of his attendance at that production.

Out of this function comes the value of theatre for youth: to cause the child to grow, to expand, to develop, to become.

Perhaps the principal area of growth made possible by this live theatre experience is the growth of the cultural level of the child. Live theatre is a combination of arts: it is literary, it is visual, it is plastic, and it is auditory. The live theatre experience is therefore the greatest teaching ground for aesthetics, and what is culture but the experience of life guided by a system of aesthetics?

Do not be misled. This goal is not a minor one, nor one of peripheral or questionable importance. It is a goal of central magnitude, for beyond making life possible, one's greatest concern must be to make that life worthwhile. By causing cultural growth in the child, by helping him to develop an aesthetic sense, the theatre helps him to seek a life with greater meaning, a life of greater understanding, a life filled with deeper joy and appreciation, a life more worth living.

But let me retreat that I may restate my argument in the broadest possible terms. The purpose of any theatre is to entertain and instruct. Its value to the community of man is proportional to how well and how broadly it carries out its function.

To me, the value of theatre for youth is that it takes this purpose seriously and has been, to thousands upon thousands of children, *the great teacher*. If those children often are not aware that they have been taught, it is because the theatre has also been successful in entertaining them, causing their enlightenment to be painless and therefore unnoticed. To be the great teacher! Is this not just reason to move mountains in the effort to further the cause of theatre for youth?

THEATRE FOR YOUTH AS AN EDUCATIONAL TOOL

Certainly, "The play is the thing." If the play itself is worthy of production, and the subsequent production is worthy of the play, then attendance at that play is a justifiable educational experience. There can, however, be far more to it than that. If a teacher should attend a play with his entire class, he then has a positive, impelling, appealing experience, common to all his students to use as an educational tool.

Further still, by checking with the school curriculum advisers, teachers, and principals, the theatre staff can correlate its choice of plays with the studies of the children who make up the audience for its productions. Along the same lines, the theatre staff can prepare and distribute to teachers and principals study guides that tie various aspects of a production to the studies of the child. Such a course of action requires time and careful effort, but it may also accrue great rewards for the theatre, the school system, and, most importantly, the child. The offerings of the theatre are no longer seen as merely entertainment but suddenly become teacher aids, educational tools, means of instructing the child in an amusing, effortless fashion. As such, the offerings of the theatre rise in prestige and are also likely to rise in popularity. The study guides, or educational material, prepared and distributed by the theatre must be broad in nature and not tied solely to theatre concerns. While it is fine to educate in terms of theatre scenery and costumes, and theatre elements such as characterization or play form, it is essential to go beyond the area of theatre and discuss broader topics. While always using the play and its contents as a basis, it is possible to bring in a multitude of conerns for study.

Let us consider some examples. The play *Young Abe Lincoln* allowed study in, among other things, the areas of art (American Primitive style), history (Lincoln's place in American and world history), English (studies of Lincoln's various writings), and human relations (the character makeup of a man of greatness and the effect on character of a series of disasters and disappointments). The play *Jack and the Beanstalk* was tied to educational material that discussed Ireland in the sixteenth century, since the play was arbitrarily set in that place and time; language characteristics, both Irish and English; folklore in general and Tennessee folklore in particular (since the play was presented in Tennessee); the various types of puppetry, with a special discussion of simple puppets for classroom use; and the scientific process of observation demonstrated by a project of raising beans, studying their growth, and comparing these ordinary beans to those magic beans the children saw sprout and grow in the play. Humperdinck's *Hansel and Gretel* allowed a discussion of music in general and opera and musical instruments in particular. It also provided a good basis for projects having to do with illustrations and the art of illustrating, creative dramatics, puppetry, literature and life in medieval Germany.

While the study guides prepared and distributed by the theatre must not be tied solely to theatrical concerns, there is nothing harmful in using them to educate children in the area of the drama. Indeed, a theatre for youth would do well to prepare a master plan whereby a student attending plays and being exposed to the educational material of the theatre would learn most facets of the theatre by the time he had completed the twelfth grade. While certain plays lend themselves strongly to this topic or that, a general plan of education can still be devised and followed. Such a plan might be:

Grades 1 and 2: Theatre behavior (including behavior during the bus ride to and from the theatre), a general introduction to theatre, creative dramatic exercises, etc.

Grades 3 and 4: The purposes and aspects of dialogue, characterization, blocking, business, and such theatrical enrichments as song, dance, music, mime, magic, puppetry, and stage combat.

Grades 5 and 6: The workers in the theatre and terms used in the theatre.

Grades 7 and 8: Such visual aspects of the theatre as scenery, costumes, lighting, makeup, and properties.

Grades 9 and 10: Play analysis—form, style, content, comparison, and criticism.

Grades 11 and 12: The history of the theatre and the art of theatre—concept, technique, unity, coherence, emphasis, selectivity, proportion, intensification, and mood.

THE GOALS OF A THEATRE FOR YOUTH

It is my belief that a cultural heritage is a necessity and every child's right. The primary goal of a theatre for youth must be to present the best in live theatre to the youth of its community in an effort to supply, or at least help to supply, that cultural heritage. This necessitates that the theatre's offerings be broad in subject matter and in style of production.

If the theatre is going to cause the child to stretch and grow, it must provide material beyond the child and his present experiences. In actuality, the whole world of emotions and experiences should be the subject matter of the theatre's presentations. While I do not advocate such things as displays of sex, violence, crime, such things do exist and the child must learn to recognize this fact and learn to deal with it. Therefore, I do not avoid sex, violence, crime, but rather try to treat them artistically, with a sense of proportion, and in a symbolic style rather than an unduly realistic one. I see nothing harmful to children in presenting sex as it is handled in the comedies of Shakespeare, for instance. In presenting *Animal Farm* to children from ten to fourteen years of age, no violent occurrence was omitted from the Nashville Children's Theatre version. However, all violence was presented symbolically, in a stylized manner, so that all violent actions became near dance passages in the play. But let us not dwell on this matter; the important idea is that all the world is subject matter for the stage.

Secondly, and of equal importance, is the idea that the youth theatre must present all styles of theatre. It is death for a youth theatre director to formulate and solidify one style of production. Since the child of most communities knows live theatre from only one source, that one source must present a variety of styles of theatre or produce a series of audience members with no idea of the versatility of theatre. For example, if a child were exposed only to the paintings of Rembrandt, he would formulate his concept of fine art out of that narrow frame of reference. Excellent as that frame of reference might be, it certainly is a restricted one. If that one painter were Picasso, on the other hand, the child's frame of reference would certainly be broader, since Picasso was far more versatile in style than was Rembrandt. It is preferable that the youth theatre director, whose works exemplify the only live theatre the children of most communities are privileged to experience, cultivate the Picasso approach to his work, attempting a versatility in his productions. Unfortunately, fame usually comes to a director who creates and polishes one style of production, which he produces to the exclusion of all other styles. Of course it is natural to try to repeat a successful style, once one has discovered how to achieve it. Also, it is natural to have a preference for one style over another, just as it is to prefer success and fame over the possibility of failure. One must remember, however, that the goal of the theatre is the important thing, and that goal centers on the child, never on the theatre workers.

ACHIEVING THE THEATRE'S GOALS

To be the great teacher: to teach culture and with it any and all information on any and all subjects—how does an organization achieve such a goal?

Initially, it does so with careful planning. It does so by thinking through its objectives, devising an orderly and systematic work plan to achieve those objectives, and instituting that plan.

Then it gives its most careful attention to the selection of scripts. Script selection should be done by a group of people chosen for their understanding of the goals of the organization and dedicated to achieving those goals. The play script is the basic element of any production, and few productions have more merit than the script being produced. The sad fact is that all too few people, even among workers in the children's-theatre movement, realize that a youth-theatre script, just as a script for the adult theatre, must have literary merit. Beyond this, a script must be entertaining and it must have pertinence.

This, then, would be a second major "how" in achieving the goals of a theatre for youth: Each year select a play reading and season selecting committee composed of the most knowledgeable and most dedicated members of the organization. The director of the organization and the director of the plays must be strongly in evidence in the work of this committee. As a personal preference, I would rather a play-reading committee present me with a larger group of approved plays from which I, as director, choose a smaller number of plays to comprise a season. I feel this preference because occasionally a perfectly worthy play may not excite or appeal to me at a given time, and if I cannot enjoy a play, I cannot communicate the joy of that play to others.

Third, the organization must select and recognize its artistic director. If a play is to be art, there must be an artist. The overall planning of the production, the master plan by which all members of a production are guided, must be the work of a recognized artist. There is no such thing as committee or group art. This does not mean that the actors, designers, and technicians cannot be creative or artists in their own right but rather that these artists create within the limits imposed by the master plan, which is the work of the master artist. Each production must have focus and major purpose, and these can be achieved only by following a master plan.

Finally, the organization must function at all times, and in all areas, in an organized manner. Preplanning and communication of plans during all phases of production are essential in order to achieve art. Truly, art does not arise out of chaos, and, while order may not manifest itself to the outside, casual observer, order must be present in the workings of a theatre or the products of that theatre will fall short of being true art. To reiterate: In order to achieve its goals, a theatre organization must know and express its goals, select basic material (plays) that support those goals, acknowledge

a master artist commissioned to achieve those goals in production, and the
organization must function in an orderly manner.

THEATRE FOR CHILDREN RATHER THAN BY CHILDREN

While one can surely find many excellent justifications for producing
theatre by children, as opposed to theatre by adults for children, theatre by
children is nevertheless a luxury for the few rather than a necessity for the
many. Beyond this, such theatre tends to be of greater benefit to the performer than the audience, and such theatre tends to be less than the best.
We are concerned here with presenting the best possible theatre to the
youth of a community, and this can be achieved only by using adults of
professional caliber to perform.

Most cities, regardless of size or location, have at best only one organization providing quality live theatre to the children of those cities and the
surrounding rural areas. This being the case, the children's theatre of an
area generally tries to serve as many children as possible. Because this is so,
the run of a successful children's play is usually a long one. In the instances
of the two producing organizations for which I have served as director,
runs of from thirty to sixty performances are the norm. It is exceedingly
difficult for a child to execute such a long and arduous run, even if his
school schedule would permit it. While I do advocate the use of child actors
in children's roles, I also find it necessary to fill such roles with several,
alternating actors.

Regardless of the length of run, however, if an organization has as its
goal the production of highly artistic theatre, it is still far preferable to use
the adult actors. That is, of course, provided the adult is of professional
caliber. This is so simply because there are few children sufficiently trained
or intuitive enough to provide the caliber of performance one must demand in order to achieve art.

I am not opposed to theatre by children. Indeed, the educational wing of
the theatre I direct presents many plays using casts of student actors. Our
goals in presenting these student productions are not the goals we are
speaking of here, however. These plays are presented free, to small audiences, and primarily for the benefit of the performers.

IN-HOUSE PERFORMANCES OR TOURS

This argument is completely dedicated to the idea of theatre as art. In
order to produce thoroughly artistic, varied theatre, it is necessary to
mount productions within a workable, well-equipped theatre plant, for
such plays are generally complexly staged plays, full of scenery, costumes,
lighting, and sound effects and full of as much magic as it is possible to
achieve.

By way of example, in *Beauty and the Beast,* as produced at the Nashville Children's Theatre, the setting featured a prince's castle made up of two silver hawks standing over sixteen feet high, and the action of the play featured the descent of the fairy godmother into the scene on the back of a butterfly. After she had dismounted, the butterfly then flew back into the sky and out of view. Humperdinck's *Hansel and Gretel,* as done at the Nashville Children's Theatre, featured a dream sequence done in the style of Czechoslovakian black light theatre, followed by the appearance of the witch riding about on her broomstick. That same company's *Animal Farm* was mounted on a multilevel stage set and utilized hundreds of slides, projected from various areas, as a backdrop and commentary to the action.

To produce this type of lavishly mounted theatre, aiming at artistry with every facet of production, it is necessary that the child come to the play. This is so because most schools and neighborhoods simply do not have facilities to support such staging. Moreover, the cost of touring a play so fully staged would be prohibitive.

Beyond this, it is advantageous that the child should travel to the play for several reasons. The experience is more exhilarating when the child leaves his customary environment to attend a special event such as a play. He therefore tends to appreciate the experience more. Secondly, if theatre for children is a training ground for adult appreciation of theatre, which it is, then part of that training is to learn one must go to the theatre. Travel to the theatre is a habit desirable to instill in the child.

For the reasons stated above, it is surely preferable to produce in-house plays. Yet, in addition to the plays produced at home, it is highly advantageous for a producing group to tour as well. Why should this be? The justifications for touring are several: 1) to reach those children who cannot, for one reason or another, come to the theatre; 2) to reach new spectators in an effort to build audiences for the in-house productions; 3) to reach an audience during special periods when that audience is unaccustomed to attending the theatre (for groups catering to schools this usually occurs during the school-year holiday periods and the summer months); and 4) for the purposes of publicity and prestige. For example, during a one-year period, in addition to its regular in-house season, the Nashville Children's Theatre presented two performances of the musical *Young Mozart* in the Eisenhower Theatre of the Kennedy Center in Washington, D.C. The play was mounted exactly as it had been done as an in-house production. The theatre presented twenty-one performances of *The Marvelous Adventures of Tyl* in twenty-one locations throughout the state of Tennessee. This production, which was designed only for touring, was a project to fill the summer months. In the fall of the year the theatre toured four companies in a special ticket sale show that included scenes, songs, dances, and mime, giving three hundred and thirty performances in one hundred and thirty-five schools to twenty-five thousand children. During the school-year period, from September through June, which is the period of NCT's major season, the school wing of the theatre toured puppet shows and demonstrations of the dramatic activities of its students. Thus, while its in-house productions were certainly the major thrust of the organization, it reached an additional thirty-five to forty thousand children through its tours. Such tours have become a necessary part of the work of the organization, for they help sustain its major season's ticket sales, carry its activities through the summer months, help it to reach thousands of children who would otherwise see no live drama, and help the theatre keep itself in the public consciousness.

AUDIENCE RANGE

A theatre for youth should have as its audience the children of its community from early youth to adulthood. Sadly, most children's theatres tend to serve only the young child. Yet, in most communities there is no other organization dedicated to serving the child during the intermediate period between young childhood and adulthood.

If a theatre for youth takes as its goal the provision of the best possible live theatre for the youth of its community, it must not fail at that goal by being shortsighted. To produce plays only for the young child would be to instill the theatregoing habit only to leave it to the community at large to keep that habit exercised. The outcome of such a procedure would be that, in most communities, from the ages of about eleven to eighteen, extremely formative years, our children and their tastes, preferences, and problems would be ignored by every live-theatre group available to them. Any habit will fade when not reinforced, and it seems pointless to create the theatregoing habit in children only to have that habit atrophy from lack of reinforcement.

SELECTING A SEASON, SOURCE OF PLAYS

Perhaps the most difficult task to be confronted by those working in the youth-theatre movement is the selection of worthwhile plays to make up a season. There is an almost unbelievable paucity of good material from which to choose, especially when one considers the many years that plays have been presented to children. For this reason it is well to employ the following eight courses of action in order to ensure a selection of worthwhile material:

(1) Encourage playwriting among your organization and in your area. Whenever anyone expresses an interest in writing a play or expresses a

good idea for a play, offer strong, positive encouragement as well as your services as technical adviser. Then schedule a series of meetings with him and indicate what work he should have completed by each meeting. People tend to respond favorably to strong encouragement and interest, so that by such a course of guiding action one will seldom lose a potential playwright, and, surprisingly, the results from these new playwrights tend to be consistently good. Since these people are members of the producing organization or familiar with it, they know the general product level and special needs of that organization. Familiarity with the special needs can often more than compensate for the new playwright's lack of experience. An organization can also sponsor a playwriting contest in an effort to encourage playwrights and acquire new scripts. Such contests generally require a goodly amount of prize money, however, and the majority of plays received from such contests tend to be unworthy of production or unsuitable for staging by the producing organization.

(2)   Therefore, should extra money be available for the encouragement of playwrights, it might more profitably be spent in commissioning new scripts from playwrights who are likely to meet the needs of your organization. By commissioning the writing of a play, you can specify subject matter, treatment of subject matter, and style of treatment, which should result in a script you can use to good effect.

(3)   Often the artistic director of an organization must take on the added task of writing or adapting material himself. As a general rule, his work requires a greater knowledge of what is needed, and the special skills required to meet those needs, than does the work of any other member of the organization. In actual practice I tend to adapt all scripts to fit the audience for which I produce. While the magnitude of my work precludes frequent attempts to create entire new scripts, the very nature of my work (producing plays to meet the needs of a special and specific audience) demands alterations to every script I do produce.

(4)   Perhaps the ideal solution to the search for new plays is to employ a company playwright or playwright-in-residence. This can be a costly practice, but if that playwright is also an actor, one may have discovered the best of all possible worlds. The actor-playwright combination is not so costly to maintain, since the position serves two functions, while at the same time the playwright who acts is constantly attuned to the reactions his material elicits. To achieve the greatest benefit from such an arrangement, the position of actor-playwright must be a long-term one, since the playwright must become thoroughly familiar with the audience he serves before he can serve that audience.

(5)   Another source of good plays for children is adult theatre. Many plays we generally think of as material for adult audiences are equally good

for children, if they are adapted slightly for younger playgoers. Since children tend to have shorter attention spans than adults, these plays usually need to be shortened. And since children have a narrower frame of reference than adults, additional explanation or simplified vocabulary sometimes needs to be employed. As children respond better to action than reflection, these adult plays need to be cut to that which moves the plot forward, eliminating descriptive passages in favor of demonstrative passages. Oftentimes, such changes need be surprisingly few in order to make an adult play most suitable for children.

(6)   It behooves a children's-theatre organization to seek material from the broadest possible range of sources. There are few publishing houses for children's plays, and it is difficult to select an exciting season from that source alone. Therefore, it is advisable to search amid such areas as Asian and European theatre, nontheatrical literature, opera, and musical comedy for good material from which to fashion plays for children.

(7)   It is also good practice to build an extensive library of plays both published and unpublished, as well as other literary material from which to create plays. The list of published plays for children is small, and the plays on that list are not always of the highest quality. Therefore, it is impractical to use publication as a mark of excellence and ignore the obscure play. It is wise to maintain an extensive library since one does not always see the value of a play on first reading. Often one is lost as to how to mount a particular property in order to make it a worthwhile endeavor. Yet, when the time is right, the style of production suggests itself, and a long-unused play script becomes the basis for a beautifully realized production.

(8)   Finally, one can sometimes develop a fine production improvisationally, relying more on an idea or story line than on a piece of written literature. Today's experimenters seem to be dealing more with pictures than words, and it is certainly possible to create an artistic play whose primary force is more visual than auditory, using a language of action rather than relying primarily on beautifully written language.

SELECTING A SEASON, VARIETY OF PLAYS

The most difficult job in selecting a season of plays is to achieve variety. Ideally, the plays should differ in the time and place they depict; they should differ in style and treatment; and they should differ in genre and in the specialty items they contain, such as music, dance, song, acrobatics, magic, and mime. They should differ in cast size, style and amount of scenery and costumes, and dependence on special effects. Finally, they should be different in intention. How tiresome it would be if all plays were heavy with message or, conversely, if all the pieces in a season were merely amusing bits of fluff. Perhaps it would be succinct and effective to list as examples of varied and balanced programs two seasons the author selected for the Honolulu Theatre for Youth.

The initial production of the first season was *The Adventures of Harlequin*, in which we took a look at early Renaissance Italy and the *commedia dell'arte* style. The set and costumes were designed after much study of the paintings of Giorgione, Giovanni Bellini, Fiorentino, Fra Angelico, and Fra Filippo Lippi. The atmosphere achieved was something quite Italian with the heady, adventurous spirit of the Renaissance. The music was authentic *commedia dell'arte* material taken from Pro Musica Antiqua recordings and the sound track of an Italian movie about a sleazy traveling *commedia* troupe, much the same as the one being portrayed. In production, we aimed to achieve a true *commedia* style, using actor involvement with the audience, slapstick, mime, song, dance, and definite character types involved in improvisation.

The second play of the season was a far more daring attempt at reconstruction, and because it was such a difficult endeavor it remains one of the highlights of my work. With the help of Mr. C. K. Huang, an authority on the Peking Opera, we presented the fairy tale *The Dragon of the Moon* in the style of the Peking Opera. It took months of study and long, arduous rehearsals, but we achieved a play filled with the special gestures and nuances of that great Oriental theatre style, with settings and costumes as literal to the style as one could possibly wish. The children who viewed the production were thrilled.

Young Abe Lincoln was the third play of the season. Although standard American musical fare, it had much of the feeling of the Emancipator's New Salem, Indiana days in it, thanks largely to the sets and costumes, inspired by Grandma Moses and other American Primitive painters. It also had its serious moments. No audience ever failed to cry at the death of Ann Rutledge, who had been so pretty and spirited in the earlier scenes of the play. Of course, it is sad to cause children to cry, but how fine it is that they could feel Lincoln's sorrow and thus understand more about the man.

With our fourth play of the season, *The Emperor's New Clothes*, we attempted a production as cold and formal as the Vivaldi, Purcell, and Haydn music that accompanied it. The setting was utterly seventeenth-century English in color and form.

With *As You Like It*, our fifth play of the season, we delved into sixteenth-century France of late northern Renaissance and early Baroque period. For pictorial inspiration we used Watteau and Fragonard, among others. The music was provided by Sibelius, Albonini, Mendelssohn, Gluck, Mozart, Vivaldi, and Beethoven. The children in the audience delighted in discovering the various aspects of love as reflected in the antics of the characters, as they also did in the various forms of combat that were added to the forest scenes of the play.

Our final show, *Kalau and the Magic Numbers,* was set in the early days of Hawaii, when Western sailors first visited the islands. The play was as historically accurate as possible and included authentic ancient hulas choreographed by Henry Pa'a and chants provided by Mrs. Mary Kawena Puku'i, one of the few authorities remaining able to reconstruct the ancient chants.

The second season opened with a rather perceptive look at friendship and faith in *The Miracle of San Fernando Mission,* a play written especially for the theatre. The setting was true in color and form to the real mission, and the costumes ranged from Mexican homespun to Spanish grandee. This serious play had its lighter moments of comedy, as well as Mexican guitar and dance numbers.

With *Ali Baba and the Forty Thieves* we brought to life one of Scheherazade's famous tales of the Arabian Nights. The setting was inspired by the architecture of Isfahan and the art of Muhammadi and Shah-Nama, to give a glimpse of the Persia of 1440–1590. The music used for the songs and dances was that of ancient Arabia and was played on instruments like those used at the time.

Young Mozart was set in the Neo-Classic and Romantic period and featured the master's own music, as well as a look at one of the first proponents of democracy and the inspirational drive that makes for great men.

Jack and the Beanstalk, our next offering, was set in medieval England in this case, although the origins of this story precede the written word and come from both England and France. Regardless of where the play is set, the story is part of our heritage, one of the myths that form part of our background and literature. It is the classic story of the boy who lives on dreams and adventure, contrasted with those who live only to possess material goods.

The Comedy of Errors, the fifth play of this second season, was set in a permanent, perspective cityscape inspired by the setting still extant at the Teatro Olympico at Vicenza, Italy. The choice of this setting necessitated that the play be set in the Italian Renaissance period, for that is when the Teatro Olympico was constructed and the permanent perspective setting installed. The choice was a happy one, however, for that period enhanced every aspect of the play, giving it a richness and beauty it would otherwise have lacked, along with a zestful quality perfect for the zany antics that occurred in the course of the play.

To end this season we chose what is to my mind the greatest of all adventure stories, *Marco Polo.* The play was set in nine stops along the way of Marco's journey, including Venice, Constantinople, Persia, and China.

The staging of the play was modern in concept, featuring the use of a space stage and slides to help tell the story of the first man to reconcile the ideas of East and West.

SELECTING A SEASON: THE CRITERIA FOR INDIVIDUAL PLAY SELECTION

When reviewing a play for possible production, the first quality I look for is the applicability of something important within that play to the lives of the children who will view it. In general, theatre is made up of problems and questions and leads to insights and answers. The play need not be blatantly moral or didactic, but it must reach and affect its audience. As with all art, the purpose of theatre is to arouse the emotions. Ideally, the emotions should be so moved as to leave a residue of agitation, conducive to subsequent thought. That is the basic purpose of all theatre, and the child must certainly be made aware of the purpose of theatre.

Beyond this, the play, or the possible production of the play, must allow the presentation of something beyond the values and knowledge the child audience presently holds; something the audience must reach toward to understand; something that challenges the interest and intellect of the audience. Without the presence of the challenge, no amount of activity on the stage can be expected to hold the reverent attention of the audience. Of course, the play must be appropriate to the child viewing it; it must complement and enhance the subject matter in which the child is interested and which he studies in his school work, but it must also possess the new and startling. One must never play down to children but always up to their potential.

If a play is worthy of being produced, it should be rich enough in material that a child viewing it is able to take ideas about art, music, history, sociology, psychology, and literature. The play should allow a production from which the child is able to fill in his concept of a period that was remote and foreign to him before seeing the play. Any play selected should be a challenge, both for the group producing it and for the group viewing it.

Beyond these considerations, there are several very practical issues to be reconciled before selecting a play. The first of these is interest. No play should be selected unless that play is capable of supporting the interest of the audience, the interest of the director, and the interest of all those others who must work on the play to make it a production. Failure to capture the interest of a cast or crew can be just as fatal to a production as failure to reach an audience.

Finally, the script must offer a practical possibility for production. If a play is beyond the ability of the director, the actors, or the technical staff, or beyond the budget of the producing organization, it had best be left un-done. A bad production of *Macbeth* is a bad production, nothing more; a production of *Peter Pan* with no flying rig could be, at the very best, a severely qualified success.

PREPARING THE PLAY FOR PRODUCTION

There are three distinct phases to the director's work in preparing a play for production, for he must function as analyst, creator, and guide. Should he neglect any of these areas, his creation will be correspondingly incomplete. Since each of these areas of work calls for different abilities within the man, it is a wonder that any director ever functions sufficiently well in all areas to be a success at his work.

Once a play has been selected for production, the work of analysis begins. It is necessary for the director at this time to discover all he can discover about the play. He must know the form of the piece, its structure, its type, school or mode, its style, and the intent of the author in writing it. As a director, I find it essential to break a play into playing scenes in order to find or create and underscore the action and flow of these scenes. I first find the core action, statement, or element of the play and then formulate how each character and each major action relates to that core—is a character or action counterpoint to the core, does it restate it, add some new dimension to it, twist it in some way, or whatever? I also seek out that which is essential introductory, developmental, or conclusive material so that I can emphasize that which is essential to an understanding of the play. Since I tend to deal with material that is somewhat sophisticated for the child, I must make certain that the intention of the piece is always clear.

Once analysis of the play is completed, the creative work begins. The first decision to be made is whether to follow the intentions and instructions of the playwright, whether to add and further develop the playwright's approach, or whether to strike out in some new direction with the piece. Even if one remains totally faithful to the intentions of the playwright, the instructions of the playwright are seldom so complete that no creative decisions need be made. There is still room for a great deal of enrichment to support his ideas. As an example, *The Wind in the Willows* depicts a character's fanatic enthusiasms and the troubles such enthusiasms cause him and his friends. These enthusiasms have to do with motion, or means of transporation. To enrich and make this theme visibly specific, the Nashville Children's Theatre production of the play featured scenes that took place in or on a moving rowboat, a bicycle built for two, an antique automobile, and a train. It further featured such effects as a shadow show on the cyclorama to depict the changing countryside through which the characters traveled, and scenery changes performed before the eyes of the audience.

Many plays, and especially so in the case of plays for children, are set in an indefinite time and location. Should I choose to produce a play of this type, I prefer to supply it with a definite time, place, and specific setting, since such an approach allows the addition of many details that enrich the telling of the tale. The story then is capable of making comment on the circumstances that caused it to unfold. Thus, *Jack and the Beanstalk* set in sixteenth-century Ireland can say something about conditions in that country at that time. A famine in that country at the time can tell us something of why Jack and his mother were so desperately hungry.

In some cases there are advantages to be found in altering the script specifications to fit your needs or the needs of your audience, as in the case of placing Shakespeare's *The Comedy of Errors* in the Italian Renaissance and featuring a permanent perspective setting. This decision allowed for the placement of all locations referred to in the action of the play on the stage throughout the play. Thus, with the addition of garden walls that were easily moved to expose the interior of Antipholous of Syracuse's house, scene flowed into scene without the necessity of any break in the action in order to change the locale.

As soon as the director has a clear idea of what he intends to do, he must consider every aspect of the show in the light of that intention. Before conferences begin with the various theatre workers, he should have in mind what he needs and desires in the way of scenery, costumes, lighting, music and sound, properties, blocking, business, and casting. While it may seem like a tall order, such a positive and thorough approach eliminates frustration, indecision, and error and results in a much smoother preparation period. In most cases I plot every movement and every piece of business after casting but before rehearsals begin. In early rehearsals these movements are conveyed to the actors, who must write them into their scripts so that they avoid lapses of memory and subsequent misunderstandings. In very rare cases, and only for some special consideration, are movements evolved improvisationally.

The director's final major creative act is in the selection of his production staff and cast of actors. Generally, production staffs tend to be long-term, while casts change with every play. Thus, the two are chosen with different criteria in mind. Versatility and temperament are especially important considerations for long-term workers. The individual play is our concern here, however, so we need not dwell on the selection of long-term staff members.

In casting a play, the director must consider the auditionee's sense of the theatrical, the personal background he brings to the play, sensitivity, imagination, audience appeal, power of projection, previous theatrical experience, and ensemble contributions, such as contrast to other cast members, unity with other cast members, and ability to cooperate. Whatever tryout method a director may prefer to use, he still must look for and weigh these considerations.

As a matter of personal preference, I use an open tryout method and have auditionees read from a script new to all, so that the conditions are as equal as possible. I ask each auditionee to read for a part at least twice so that he may become familiar with the piece in my presence. I also give directions as to how I would like the piece interpreted for the second reading so that I can witness the actor's ability to take direction and alter his interpretation. During the audition I look primarily for the actor's personal aura—that is, the type of person he projects unconsciously by nature. If the actor is inexperienced, I tend to cast to the aura the actor naturally conveys. If he is experienced, I cast an actor capable of projecting the aura desired. Thus, I am assured that the actor will succeed in portraying the type of character necessary, and rehearsal time can be spent on detail, polish, and nuance. On very rare occasions, when an actor cannot function at an open tryout, I hold a further, closed tryout.

One other word on tryouts is in order. Always make clear to all audi-tionees the total commitment involved and urge any auditionee unable to meet the full obligation to so state on his tryout card. By utilizing this simple procedure one will seldom be forced to replace an actor unable to meet the full commitment.

With the completion of planning and casting, the director shifts into the third phase of his work—that of guide. Now, he must call on his powers to cooperate and communicate, giving free rein to others to create within the bounds of the plan he has prepared.

In dealing with designers and technical workers I use a system of regu-larly scheduled group meetings in order to ensure a unity of style among the various aspects of the play, along with frequent personal contact with each worker to see that he is proceeding along the lines specified. By this method it is possible to ensure the completion of a project as desired while avoiding costly and demoralizing mistakes. Frequency of contact is essen-tial, however, in order to communicate and coordinate all details.

In rehearsing the actors I always follow a procedure that I have found works well for me. At the first cast meeting, every actor receives a cast list that gives all names, addresses,and telephone numbers of those involved, a rehearsal schedule listing all rehearsals and what we will attempt to achieve at each rehearsal, a performance schedule listing all performances and possible extension performances, and a property list that includes all prop-erties and who is to use them. I then display and explain all set and costume designs and describe the plans for lights, music, and sound. I provide the actors with a copy of the educational material for the play so that they are aware of what we are trying to say with the play, and I discuss each characterization with the cast. The rehearsal schedule I employ is as follows:

FIRST REHEARSAL: First reading and discussion, costume measurements taken.

SECOND, THIRD, AND FOURTH REHEARSALS: Blocking rehearsals. The play is taken sequentially in twelve-page segments.

FIFTH, SIXTH, AND SEVENTH REHEARSALS: Business and details, again sequentially in twelve-page segments.

EIGHTH, NINTH, AND TENTH REHEARSALS: Characterization in twelve-page segments.

ELEVENTH REHEARSAL: First half of play performed without scripts.

TWELFTH REHEARSAL: Second half of play performed without scripts.

THIRTEENTH REHEARSAL: Costume parade—at which time all costumes are worn and displayed before finishing touches are made.

FOURTEENTH REHEARSAL: Full run-through of play without scripts.

FIFTEENTH AND SIXTEENTH REHEARSALS: Run-throughs with all properties, timing and pacing.

SEVENTEENTH, EIGHTEENTH, AND NINETEENTH REHEARSALS: Technical rehearsals, full run-throughs with all aspects of production except costumes and makeup.

TWENTIETH, TWENTY-FIRST, AND TWENTY-SECOND REHEARSALS: Full-dress rehearsals.

By employing such a specific and planned rehearsal schedule, I and every actor involved in the play know what it is we must accomplish with each rehearsal. While the above detailed rehearsal schedule holds true for every play we produce, it is added to whenever a play has special requirements. For instance, rehearsals for musicals feature three rehearsals devoted to learning the music before the blocking of the show begins. Then, music and dance rehearsals are interspersed between the blocking, business, and characterization rehearsals so that all elements of the play still come together at the time of the first run-through rehearsal. Utilizing this schedule for rehearsals, all shows tend to peak at the time of the first dress rehearsal. We then concentrate on maintaining that peak and polishing minor flaws during the remaining rehearsals. I never worry about a play falling from its peak level, since I deal with professionals conditioned to maintaining a peak level of performance for a long run (from thirty to sixty performances). The far more important goal is to open the show with all involved feeling a strong sense of confidence and control.

During the period that I, as director, act as guide, I use projected audience response as my major criterion. When considering any detail of design or action, I try to view it as the audience will view it. If I anticipate that the audience will understand an action, and further understand why that action was performed, and agree it was well to perform that action in the way it was performed, then the action is good. Whether or not I, personally, like the action is of no importance. As a matter of course, I try not to interfere in any way with the creative process of those under my guidance. My aim is to achieve an atmosphere in which art can flourish as a positive experience. This does not mean that the ideas of others are not guided, altered, or rejected, but these others are treated thoughtfully and given some reason for change or rejection. That reason usually has to do with audience response.

While I try for a different approach and a different style of production with every play I produce, I do consistently aim for a richness of production values. It has become second nature to utilize these resources when working in a fully equipped theatre with a large body of technicians. Shows calling for little more than actors and audience are generally reserved for the summer season. The old adages "A simple story simply told" and "Less is more" are very appealing to me, and I do apply them to the treatment of the main story line. Yet, far more appealing is the play richly mounted. I expect lights to do more than merely illuminate because they are capable of doing more. I expect scenery to do more than block the audience's view of the backstage, because scenery design is an art and I ask the theatre artist to produce art. I expect costumes to do more than cover the body.

It has been argued that children do not need fully mounted plays because they imagine what is lacking. This may be so, but I know that children have limited frames of reference and thus I endeavor to supply the child's imagination with enough material to act as a point of reference and catalyst to stimulate the process of imagination.

CONCLUSION

It is natural to appreciate and indulge in the dramatic. Dramatic productions presented live to children can be powerful educational tools, especially so since they appeal to children. By preparing educational materials to accompany its plays, a children's-theatre organization can greatly increase the value of its product. For this to be true, however, the product of the children's-theatre organization must be broad in scope, highly artistic in quality, and created within an ordered framework.

MISCELLANY

(1) I find that children respond well to plays that are forty-five minutes to an hour in length. Children can maintain attention for this period of

time, and they experience no physical problem in remaining seated for this period of time. Moreover, it requires no more time than this to tell most stories well.

(2) Consequently, I work with scripts of no more than one thousand lines, since one thousand lines generally can be performed in one hour, and scripts of no more than thirty-six pages, since it takes thirty-six pages to contain one thousand lines.

(3) I have experienced a growing preference for what is essentially a thrust-stage playing area. I like to keep the action close to the children, yet I like the action to appear in a full setting, or, preferably, a series of full settings. While the stage with which I work is of the proscenium style, I am constantly causing the playing area to be built out in one way or another and the action of the play to spill out beyond the confines of the proscenium.

(4) In actuality, I prefer to think of what I produce as family theatre rather than theatre for youth or children's theatre, since the production tends to be of value and interest to the adult as well as the child. Otherwise, I prefer "theatre for youth" to "children's theatre," since what we know as children's theatre has tended to ignore all but the very young child.

(5) I have great respect for traditional children's material treated traditionally. On the other hand, I delight in traditional material being given a pertinent, modern twist. Surely, there is room for more than one approach to any given subject.

(6) I steer clear of jumping on the bandwagon of any one style of theatre or the style that happens to be in current vogue. While I am willing to experiment in any style I believe can be valid, at least for some specific project, I tend to avoid participation plays, since I favor theatre as art over theatre as a game, therapy, equalizer, or whatever it is participatory theatre tries to achieve. Story theatre can sometimes serve a great purpose in telling a story of broad scope, although it tends to be theatre devoid of magic and beauty. Chamber theatre, on the other hand, is pure delight.

The Meeting Center. The home of the Empire State Youth Theatre Institute, State University of New York. Photo: Office of General Services Public Information Office Tower Building, Empire State Plaza, Albany, N.Y. 12228

Patricia Snyder has the distinction of directing the first American children's-theatre production to perform in the Soviet Union. Her 1974 production of *The Wizard of Oz* in the Soviet Union was given under the auspices of the State University of New York at Albany, where Professor Snyder was a member of the theatre faculty. She is currently director of the Empire State Youth Theatre Institute, a professional company established to tour plays to schools and communities in the area.

Patricia Snyder received her bachelor's degree from the State University of New York at Albany and her M.F.A. degree from Syracuse University. She has taught on all levels, has traveled extensively, visiting theatres for children in various parts of Europe, and has received numerous honors and awards. She was given a special Recognition Citation by the Children's Theatre Association of America for her organization of the 1972 International Congress (ASSITEJ), which took place in Albany.

She was appointed to the New York State Education Arts and Humanities Planning Committee for the Annual Statewide Conference and to the Education Board of the Saratoga Performing Arts Center; and she has been a United States delegate to ASSITEJ conferences in the Hague and Venice. Patricia Snyder is one of the best-informed persons in this country on the subject of children's theatre throughout the world.

THE EMPIRE STATE
YOUTH THEATRE INSTITUTE

The First State-Mandated
Educational Theatre for Children
in America

13

PATRICIA SNYDER

*L*ive theatre in America may be suffering from a life-threatening disease because too few theatre artists and crafts people are willing to give their best effort to theatre for young people. The performers, directors, designers, and ideas that have been rejected by the "big time" theatre are allowed to sink into children's theatre, and the young American audience gets second-rate theatre for its first theatrical experience. Aren't we perpetuating second-rate theatre by letting this happen? And aren't we passing up our *best* opportunity to develop a lasting American theatre audience?

There was some concern in the 1960s that theatre in America was dead. Contemporary American theatre for young people could be administering the *coup de grace* to live theatre in America.

If we are to keep the unique art of live theatre alive in America, today's young audiences must experience only the best when it comes to the theatre. If great theatre is not given to our young people, there isn't much chance that they will demand and support great theatre when they are adults.

We need a new credo for children's theatre, and I will propose it here: Children's theatre is simply *no good* if it isn't *good theatre*.

A new credo is fine, but are there any practical means to implement it? In the American 1970s theatre in general is hard pressed to maintain a standard of excellence, mostly because everything costs more. The gap between production costs and box-office income has widened, and theatre benefactors (public and private) have become more stringent and skeptical.

Therefore, perhaps the best way to ensure quality and longevity is to *institutionalize* theatre—children's theatre—in a very special way.

New York State was a pioneer in government assistance to the arts. The New York State Council on the Arts was the predecessor to its federal counterpart, the National Endowment for the Arts. Today, all states have established similar councils on the arts and/or humanities, and there is in those states at least a slight predisposition to giving some priority to good theatre for young people, such as the Children's Theatre Company of Minneapolis.

What has happened in New York is perhaps years away in other states, but New York has established what amounts to an official—though autonomous—state-created theatre organization: The Empire State Youth Theatre Institute.

The Empire State Youth Theatre Institute had its beginning in the early Seventies, when the New York State Commission on Cultural Resources observed that "we have a dichotomy between two vast systems of education —our cultural institutions and our schools. Neither system communicates with the other very much. Our artists, scientists, and historic societies all exist in our communities separate and apart from the formal educational institutions—our schools. This is both detrimental to the education of our children as well as an expense we can ill afford."[1]

The State University of New York at Albany had been operating a modest program in Children's Theatre and Creative Dramatics for five years when the Cultural Resources Commission delivered its report. One of the results of the SUNY at Albany program was to make the cultural resource of the University's Theatre Department directly available to Albany-area elementary and secondary schools through a series of touring productions. The State University of New York Chancellor, Ernest L. Boyer, decided to take up the challenge inherent in the Cultural Resources Commission Report by proposing an expansion of the Albany program to the statewide level.

Working with New York State Senator William Conklin, the State University developed legislation to amend the state's education law by creating the Empire State Youth Theatre Institute. The Institute was proposed as being "under the jurisdiction and control of the State University" and mandated to:

1. establish in the Empire State Plaza an arts and cultural program
    for the youth and educators of New York State, to include the
    visual and performing media;

1. New York State Commission on Cultural Resources, "Arts in the Schools, Patterns for Better Education."

2. offer New York State elementary and secondary-school teachers in-service training in the use of the arts as a community resource and as a complement to all other areas of education;
3. offer accredited internships in "arts for children" to students being trained as teachers and artists of both public and private institutions of higher learning;
4. offer opportunities for college-level student directors, actors, and designers from public and private institutions to direct, perform, and design in the arts for children in a professional atmosphere;
5. offer guidance and consultation to children's arts programs in schools and colleges throughout the state;
6. stimulate children's arts programs in regional centers throughout the state;
7. serve as the nucleus for a professional children's theatre company and arts center;
8. offer touring programs in children's arts to elementary and secondary schools throughout New York State;
9. develop arts audiences for the future by serving as a stimulus to children with little or no experience in the arts who visit Empire State Plaza.

The legislation also required the state of New York to provide facilities for the Empire State Youth Theatre in Albany's Empire State Plaza in The Meeting Center, a convention complex that includes two theatres. While the facility does not *make* the program, the arts, like the sciences, require a well-equipped laboratory. The Empire State Youth Theatre Institute's laboratory is well equipped, with its own scene shop, costume, jewelry and millinery shops, rehearsal room, conference and music rooms, classroom, and general offices.

The act creating the Institute was passed unanimously by the 1974 session of the New York state legislature and signed into law by the Governor in May of that same year. Thus, the concept of the Empire State Youth Theatre Institute as a state-supported children's art educational center became part of the education law in New York State.

The legislative process was followed by a two-year developmental period, during which the State University of New York provided funding for a small staff. It was during this time that some of the most respected names in theatre, the arts, and education—Donald Oenslager, Richard P. Leach, T. Edward Hamilton, Arthur Foshay, John Houseman, Cyril Ritchard, and Norris Houghton—were consulted for their advice regarding the Institute's program structure as well as serving to recommend designers and directors for the initial season. Both John Houseman and Cyril Ritchard lent their support in appearing in the media as spokesmen for the Youth Theatre. Soon the basic framework for the first contemporary government-supported children's theatre began to emerge.

The Empire State Youth Theatre Institute encompasses a high-quality professional program serving the serious theatre student, the child and student audience of New York State, and the elementary or secondary teacher in search of comprehensive in-service training toward the use of the arts as a teaching tool.

The Youth Theatre Institute facilitates a statewide creative laboratory and showcase for graduate and undergraduate students of theatre and the associated arts and humanities from public and private campuses around the state. There is a released-time, career-oriented program in theatre for qualified high school students.

The student's exposure to theatre in the controlled environment of a classroom is not realistic. There is a security in a classroom that is absent in the outside world. Utilizing the performing arts as a method or "learning tool," enfolding lifelong situations through drama and providing the opportunity for involvement and discussion, provides more realistic and meaningful experiences.

Through this approach children are exposed to the values of the various classes of society, in addition to their own. In essence, the Institute attempts to become a microcosm of life within the framework of theatre and the arts.

Basic to the Youth Theatre staff is the teacher-artist ensemble. The teacher-artist ensemble consists of arts faculty and professional actors. These persons function as both practitioners and teachers of their particular specialty. They were selected on the merits of accomplishment in their field and not necessarily on the basis of academic credentials. The teacher-artists perform in the Institute's season of plays for youth as directed by a member of the ensemble or visiting directors. They also work in the Institute's programs designed specifically for student interns and teachers of elementary and secondary schools. This ensemble participates in pre- and post-performance discussions and activities with members of the audience. The ensemble size is supplemented by interns from private and public institutions of higher learning on a per-semester basis. The full ensemble represents all specialities of the theatre, incorporating dance, music, and the spoken word. In addition, ensemble members have demonstrated an ability to teach and work with young people. It should be mentioned that the entire Institute staff, including the administrators, are required to participate actively in the Institute's producing program. For example, the educational coordinator may also create costumes for the ensemble productions or lead a small post-production group discussion with the audience in a given school. This may be the ideal, but we believe that, through the combination of teacher and artist, a great number of interdisciplinary goals can be achieved.

One of the Youth Theatre's primary functions is to operate a touring program that is available to all of the elementary and secondary schools in New York State. The touring program includes fully staged productions of a series of theatrical productions and accompanying workshops conducted in a three-day residency in the schools. During each residency the teacher-artists live in the students' community, present at least two or more of the Institute's six productions, and conduct workshops that occur before and after each performance.

The purpose of these productions is to serve as vehicles for initiating both the teachers and students into a discovery process of the essentials of human communication. Through the processes basic to the workshops, participants examine values and interrelationships involved in:

—making choices
—identifying alternatives
—being aware of consequences
—dealing with peers and with "different" people
—forming attitudes
—examining motives
—exploring the dualities inherent in natural existence (life/death, light/dark, love/hate) and examining both their symbolic and actual roles in life, thus clarifying the integral relationships between the principles of the nature of beauty and morality
—through an examination of words, movement, motivation, character projection, and the evoking of emotions, understand the value of dramatic communication as it extends and expands cognitive thinking.

In addition to the workshops guided by the Youth Theatre's teacher-artists, materials and suggestions are available to the staff of each school as an encouragement to further pursue the methods, themes, and philosophies that emerge from the process.

The Youth Theatre's productions were chosen as a cross-sectional representation of styles of dramatic communication, which can appeal to a wide age range, and to focus upon concepts and attitudes relevant to the development of values and an understanding of societal and cultural heritage.

While the plays and basic workshop structures, because of the residency time limitations, deal specifically with fundamental personal inter-relationships—peer and familial—discussion groups and participating classroom teachers will be guided toward an awareness of the interdependence, not only of individuals, but also of communities, nations, cultures and races. Humanistic values, through a holistic view, encourage the individual to relate positively to environment, society, and culture by bringing into a unified picture the functioning of the physical body, emotions, thought, culture and social expression.[2]

The basic goal of the residencies, therefore, is to bring about an understanding of the human race as a kind of "extended family," an acceptance of the fact that each individual is part of a universal ecosystem—that, like a pebble tossed into a pond, the individual tossed into earthly existence sends ripples, disturbances, effects that are felt far beyond his or her immediate environment. The goal of each individual should be, in this context, to become aware of his or her responsibility within the family, community, society, culture, and to become able and eager to contribute, to learn from and enjoy the limitless possibilities for accomplishment of all members of the global family as well as to develop and explore his or her own potential.

SUGGESTED THREE-DAY INSTITUTE TOURING PROGRAM

The time and space limitations imposed by each school necessarily affect the format of the workshops and the amount of experimentation and discussion that can be done. The following plan is based on the assumption that the Institute will be allowed the seventh, eighth, and ninth grades (approximately three hundred students) during three full school days.

The regular teachers of these students are visited up to a month earlier by a member of the Institute staff and participate in a special workshop that prepares them to participate in the workshops for the students and will enable and encourage them to pursue further, in their regular classes, the themes that emerge from the productions and workshops, especially those focusing on scientific, political, and cultural tensions of various aspects of the workshops.

Day 1:

Morning workshop

Goals:
—to introduce students to the concept of "role playing" in everyday life
—to acquaint students with the teacher-artists as individual human beings who earn a living by "playing roles"

2.   Elaine Frankonis, Educational Coordinator.

—to acquaint students with the themes and background of the production scheduled for the afternoon

Activities:

Depending on the number of home rooms in grades 7, 8, and 9,
the teacher-artists will divide up so that there is at least one teacher-
artist and one regular teacher in each class.

The regular teacher and the teacher/artist will, through an introductory dialogue, provide information about the teacher-artist, will
identify the "roles" he or she plays in the two productions the students
will view, and will initiate a discussion on "role playing." Purpose: to
enable the students to discover that they themselves play different
roles in the classrooms from those they play in the principal's office;
different when they are with friends than with family and that others
respond to these "roles."

The discussion is led back to the idea of "role playing" in a play,
and the basic characters of the play scheduled for the afternoon,
Winterthing, are briefly introduced.

Using maps, charts, etc., available in the individual school, the
regular teacher explains the geographical setting; the influence of
weather and seasonal changes; the concept of germination in darkness; the dualities essential to natural existence, such as light/dark,
night/day, war/peace, addition/subtraction, leading students to discover that dualities or opposites exist as an integral part of every
discipline and indeed in every person and every society.

The discussion with the class should be led in the direction of becoming
aware that individuals play "roles" and that how well we communicate with
others depends on how we "come on" to them, how well we understand
and accept our own dualities.

Class discussion should arrive at the fact that observers initially respond
to an individual as a result of the "role" he or she plays, the "impression" he
or she makes.

Day 1:

Afternoon performance

If there is time, depending on the school's schedule, the teacher-
artist will either field questions from the entire group as they remove
their makeup on stage or will return to the classes with the students to
do the same. Discussions should be led to focus on the characters of
the play: Did the students like or dislike them? Were the characters

one-dimensional? Identifiable as "types"? Realistic? How did they
function as a group? Did they understand and accept one another?
What roles did each play within the group?

Day 2:

Morning workshop

Goals:
—to lead the students into an evaluation of the play in terms of
   choices made by characters; concept of the family unit; analysis of
   consequences; roles of individuals within a group; students' attitudes toward characters; developing students' awareness of cold
   and warm, light/dark, winter/spring as symbolic and real dualities
—to review and expand on the students' understanding of myths and
   legends
—to provide students with an opportunity to "role play" characters of
   their own choosing in the context of a legend or myth of their own
   creation

Activities:

   A teacher-artist other than the one who worked with the group
previously is introduced by the regular teacher. The teacher-artist
initiates a discussion of *Winterthing*, guiding student awareness to
areas indicated in the goals and continuing to answer questions not
covered after the performance.
   Students break up into groups of about ten each. Their assignment
is to evolve an original myth, create and develop the characters of the
myth. Each student will then be responsible for choosing one character to portray and for developing this character's personality, mood,
body movements, voice quality, and attitudes toward the other characters and to the plot.
   Each group will then, with guidance from the teacher-artist, improvise a short scene, using the myths and characters it has developed,
stressing the individual character's influence on the mechanics of the
group.
   There will be a discussion by the class after each group's "performance," regarding the appropriateness of the myth or legend, the
class's attitudes toward the characters that were created, and the ways
in which the characters interrelated.

Day 2:

Afternoon workshop

Goals:

—to restate the concept of "role playing"

—to introduce the students to *The Miracle Worker,* the play they will see the next morning

—to develop an understanding in the students that role playing is a form of communication

—that communication takes place through the senses

—that sensory deprivation makes communication frustrating and sometimes almost impossible

Activities:

A third teacher-artist will be present in the room. The regular teacher will be seated, eyes closed. The teacher-artist will be trying to communicate, unsuccessfully, with the other teacher, who is apparently deaf, mute, and blind. All this is occurring as the students enter the room.

Eventually, the teacher-artist should bring the class to discussing what is going on.

The teacher-artist then asks for volunteers to come up and try to communicate with the "deaf, mute, and blind" teacher. Discussion should evolve on how to go about it. The students should try to get the "impaired" teacher to do something simple, such as hold a pencil and make marks on a paper. The point should be made that if someone has never "sensed" a pencil or paper, he or she could not possibly know what to do with them. It will be obvious, eventually, that the sense of touch is the only way such a person can communicate.

This discussion should lead into an introduction to *The Miracle Worker,* with the teacher-artist and "recovered" teacher providing information about the period in history, the attitudes toward handicapped people at that time, the kinds of institutions into which such people were placed, and the kinds of experiences the ill, the elderly, and the handicapped were exposed to.

The conclusion from the class will hopefully be that, when one or more senses are impaired, communication is frustrated, because we use our senses to communicate. We also use our senses to "play" roles and to interpret other people's roles.

Discussion should be steered toward the question of which sense is the most valuable. There will be various opinions. Since we communicate so much with our bodies, as was evident in the role playing, the sense of sight might be considered the most useful means of getting information about our environment and about other people. The teacher-artist will refer to role-playing exercises and the importance of sight, suggesting that sometimes actions *do* speak louder than words.

Teacher-artist pantomimes, suggesting a "role," a personality, through actions. The class will then discuss the "role" and pantomime as a means of communication.

Students break up into smaller groups, with each group evolving a pantomime based on the actions and reactions of a group of people, one of which is deaf, mute, and blind. Each participant must choose and play out one specific "attitude" toward a handicapped person.

Class discussion after each group presentation, focused on the values inherent in the ways in which each individual reacted to the handicapped character as well as in this character's response.

Day 3:

Morning performance of *The Miracle Worker*

Day 3:

Afternoon workshop

With yet another teacher-artist present as a guide, the students break up into small groups to develop improvisations based on group or family situations provided in written form by the Institute. Each group will choose one situation that will be based on a problem of one member and his/her relationship to the rest of the group—i.e., one situation will involve an alcoholic parent, another a mentally retarded child. The point of the exercise is to encourage the students and teachers to so empathize with the character they portray in the scene that they will each think, feel, respond, and act in manners appropriate to that character. If time permits, roles may be exchanged so that, for example, the individual who at one point plays the role of the frustrated, angry child of an alcoholic parent will also have the opportunity to view and act on the situation from the point of view of that parent. In this way the individual will learn to identify with the problems of another human being, to understand that, while each individual tends to create his or her own reality, the existence of one member of a group such as a family is bound up with the existence of others. With the time remaining in the workshop period, students will be encouraged to ask any questions relative to any aspects of the three-day program. The teacher-artist will also encourage discussion of how the techniques used during the workshops might be applied in their regular classes—for example, students in history classes can attempt to emphasize and even recreate the individual lives and emotions of people in various periods of history. Science classes might be interested in discussing myths, both old and modern, their origins and eventual deaths, and their effects on cultures and various lives.

Even after the workshops are completed, the resources of the Institute will be available on request to all interested teachers, even those whose classes were not a part of the three-day program. Hopefully, the experiences of the participants will encourage other teachers to seek out teacher-training workshops in the arts and humanities offered by the Institute.

PARTICIPANTS

Audience (Participants)

The composition of the audience whom the Youth Theatre Institute serves is best described in four major categories:

1. *Student Interns*

    Student interns are:

    a. Any student enrolled in a public or private institution of higher learning in New York State. Student interns will be admitted to study and work at the Institute by recommendation from their resident compuses, followed by audition and interview at the Institute. Following acceptance, the interns will work and study in their area of interest. Through consultation with college and university officials, and students as well as faculty in both private and SUNY units, it is indicated that the Institute's creative laboratory will serve

    a. Students whose major field is not theatre, but desire to work in an artistic setting to enhance their understanding of their own area of study.

    b. Students who desire to pursue a career in the theatre.

The Institute will not offer a degree program; rather, it will function within a system by which the intern's work is validated by the Institute and subsequently credited to his transcript by the intern's resident campus. The validation procedure will be designed to meet the requirements of individual intern's resident campuses.

The student constituency of the Institute will probably be divided into four broad categories:

—those from SUNY units

—those from private and out-of-state colleges and universities

—those from other agencies and institutions (e.g., elementary and secondary schools, therapeutic agencies, hospitals and state agencies).

—those without institutional affiliation.

Students will elect to intern at the Institute for a program ranging from no credit to a full semester's credit. The intern's workload will generally be commensurate to the amount of credit he seeks. Each intern will prearrange his program at the Institute in consultation with the Institute staff and appropriate officers at his resident campus.

Student interns will be invited to continue at the Institute so long as they continue to demonstrate substantial growth toward artistic excellence. Interns will be evaluated on a semester basis, and the number of interns will be limited according to the availability of professional staff.

Individualized programs will be devised for interns at the Institute; however, some basic theatre arts-and-crafts courses will be offered on a regular basis by the professional staff. These courses will, in most cases, parallel courses offered in theatre programs at other institutions so that an intern might complete some requirements toward his major sequence at his resident campus while at the Institute.

As an adjunct to their internship program, interns will occasionally be required to function as auxiliary staff at the Institute as assigned by the various professional staff responsible for the operation of the Institute's programs. They will be compensated for their services through a modest stipend arrangement.

2. *Elementary- and secondary-school teachers* will receive:
    a.   in-service training in the use of arts as a community resource and as a complement to all other areas of education. Teachers can receive credit toward graduate degrees through the Institute;
    b.   guidance and consultation in planning children's arts programs;
    c.   touring programs in children's arts.

3. *Youth and the community in general* will be the third component of the Institute's audience. In addition to the touring program, performances will be held in the theatres at the Empire State, which is the home base for the Institute. Here, the opportunity for field trips to the state's capitol and the state's museum can be incorporated with attendance at a theatrical production. Tours through the facility will be scheduled along with a discussion session with the Institute ensemble after each production.

4. *Senior citizens and handicapped citizens in general* will be recruited for ancillary Institute participants, especially in the areas of costuming, stagecraft, box office, and ushering. A special effort will be made to incorporate this last group into Institute activities in order to achieve a microcosm of life within the framework of theatre and the arts.

EVALUATION OF PROJECT

The Empire State Youth Theatre Institute is committed to continuing, searching evaluation of its programs and policies. The Institute also seeks valid and reliable assessment of programs in the arts. Also, the Institute invites nationally known authorities and practitioners in the arts to observe the Institute's programs in action and asks these specialists for guidance toward improvement of the programs.

Throughout the initial stages of the project (1975–77) and thereafter, the Institute has continued to conduct both formative and summative evaluation of programs. The Institute works with an interdisciplinary team of evaluators from the Statutory Colleges of Cornell University (Ithaca, New York). This team has worked with the Institute staff to develop an evaluation design specifically tailored to the Institute's goals and program.

Of course, the audience/participants will play a large role in shaping, evaluating, and reshaping the program. A complete set of pre- and post-production taped interviews with audience/participants will be recorded, as well as a questionnaire designed for the school's teachers and administrators. In this last instance, we are eager to gain insight into the teachers' and administrators' observations concerning the effectiveness of our program.

All evaluative results will be utilized in the preparation of the next season of Institute offerings. The curriculum goals will change with the new offerings of each season, although some productions will be kept in repertory.

Pre- and post-season testing will take place in participating schools. Here it is important to note that some school administrators would like to hear that our program will raise scores on standardized tests, but we caution against the likelihood of such results. Even the question of the Institute's contribution to audience development will be difficult to document within a two-year period. We do believe, however, that results can be measured over a ten-year period of research and documentation.

There is much to be studied and discovered before we can lay positive claim to dramatic results. But if we can gain the support of school principals for an active arts-in-education program in their schools through developing a healthier school with motivated students and well-prepared, enthusiastic teachers in a typical program, we will be taking a great step toward enlarging our knowledge of the world and developing a better understanding of ourselves and others.

Production of *Harlequinade* by The Acting Company of The Young Peoples Theatre of City Center, New York directed by Marjorie Sigley.

Marjorie Sigley has attracted attention on both sides of the Atlantic for her innovative work in children's theatre. Her preparation includes a background in education and the theatre arts. She has a diploma from Goldsmith's College of London University and studied at the University of Manchester, where she was named a Fellow in Drama.

She began directing and writing professionally at the Mermaid Theatre in London in 1960, while at the same time lecturing for the London County Council. The formation of an experimental theatre group and her position —teaching mime and movement at the City Literary Institute in London— offered her an opportunity to create new instructional methods. Indeed, her concept of theatre for children was developed at this time and was based on her belief in the practical use of theatre techniques in the classroom.

In 1970 Marjorie Sigley came to New York to join the faculty of the Herbert Berghof Studio. It was then that she formed the basis of a new company of actors, who were to become the first City Center Young People's Theatre performer-teachers. For the next four years the theatre district of Manhattan was to witness busloads of school children arriving daily to participate in the dramatic activities downstairs at City Center. In 1975 this highly successful enterprise became an independent organization.

In the following article Marjoire Sigley describes her philosophy of theatre for children and the methods she has found to work most successfully.

CHILDREN AND THE THEATRE

A Personal Story

14

MARJORIE SIGLEY

*C*hildren and theatre! I suppose the first question to ask is: "How do you bring them together?" or "Who brings the theatre to children?" or "Who takes children to the theatre?" then "What do they see?"

Thought: How does it begin, one's interest in this most magical of art forms?

Recently, sitting in the auditorium of the Olivier Theatre in London, I couldn't help being more interested in the audience than in the performance. At long last the British have achieved their National Theatre and at a time when economic stress could not be worse and everything would seem to be against it. The South Bank has become a Mecca for all—and there they were as mixed and varied a group of people as one would wish to find in an audience. But how did they get there? What were they seeking that was special and different in this place called a theatre? What had made them struggle through the mad chaos of London's traffic to join in a cultural ritual when they could be rushing home to the known "delights" of the television? A big question! I know why I was there; I love the theatre. I always have, and I am proud that it is my profession. But how does it begin, one's interest in the theatre? Each one of us has our own explanation and mine is simple.

I was born in Buxton, a small resort town in the Peak National Park of Derbyshire, England. The town has a delightful opera house, a theatre, a concert hall, and a cinema—all for a population of twenty thousand people, and in 1976 the buildings are all still there. However, since I was a child,

TV has wrought its effect, and audiences in towns like these are no longer what they were. When people do manage to tear themselves away from their TV, it is mostly to socialize at bingo, whist drives, and dances. Plays, opera, and serious music are for the minority. Indeed, they need to be subsidized, as they cannot pay their way. So the theatre has a short season, the concerts are infrequent, and the opera is in Manchester.

What a pity! For the weekly repertory system of the Buxton Playhouse and the tours of major theatre and opera companies, like the Old Vic, were what I grew up on. While I was still in school I had a knowledge of plays, writers, and actors that even a seasoned playgoer today, living in a big city, would be envious of. By the time I was sixteen I was familiar with most of the plays of Shaw, O'Casey, Coward, Priestly, Rattigan and Emlyn Williams, I had seen at least twenty of Shakespeare's plays, the more popular ones several times; I had been introduced to the works of Molière, Chekhov, Ibsen, Thornton Wilder, Arthur Miller, and other international writers and had heard Sybil Thorndyke talk about her life to an audience of us school children in between a matinee and an evening performance. She inspired me to such an extent that I wanted to leave home immediately and join the theatre.

Join! A very important choice of word in this context. Whatever part of the theatrical scene you undertake you must always join your effort to those of others to bring about the final happening, and whatever you as a company have created must be received by another group of people, the audience, to make the whole thing complete.

These are the simple and fundamental reasons why I believe theatre to be an essential part of our existence, our right and our heritage.

Creation, interpretation, collaboration, and *cooperation.*

Nobody is going to force you to buy a ticket and go to a theatre. One needs a motivation to do most things, though people do seem forced by some unknown power to buy a TV set and automatically turn it on. So what is it that makes you, or me, or any individual, *want* to go to the theatre? As a child I found it an adventure, a place where my rich world of imagination joined others in the satisfaction of the dramatic. I was lifted into another place. I loved reading, playing the piano, and going to the cinema. From the age of eleven I was crazy about films, but the theatre was always in another place in my mind. I didn't come from a family that had any particular interest in the arts. I wasn't discouraged, but neither was I encouraged. Whatever it was that happened to me happened to me, myself. I got the fever and I've had it ever since.

Now the point of all this is not to boast but to show that availability is essential. If I hadn't had all that on my doorstep, I might never have gone to London and pursued a career as I did. If we want our children to grow up involved in the arts, we have to make sure that the arts are there, regularly and continuously, and at a price that does not create an elitism. We must also ensure that the quality is high and the guiding spirits are men and women of vision and integrity.

A tall order!

Thought: Perhaps the arts in general have become too complicated. If it were all as easy and delightful as J. B. Priestley's *Good Companions,* it would be wonderful. There seems to be too much money involved these days.

It wasn't sensible to think about the theatre as a job when I went to school.

"What do you want to do?"

"I want to work in the theatre!"

"That's not sensible! You can't earn your living that way!"

It wasn't sensible then and it isn't now, and the chances of making a living are still slender, but you don't do it for that reason. Try telling your parents that! You won't get far in most cases.

I had been very well educated musically and was very good at sports, so somewhere at the back of my parents' mind was the firm idea that I would make a good music or gym teacher. Being a happy and rather carefree adolescent, I never really thought what I might do. It had all been prearranged, and it wasn't until I had been out of college for several years that I had the courage to leave a secure job for the joy, pleasure, hard work, and uncertainty of the theatre.

Thought: It never occurred to me that I should or could go against the wishes of my mother.

My mother has a strong conviction that one should serve society to the best of one's ability. To her, teaching is a highly respected vocation; teachers are leaders of society, and they are there for forty years! No risks, no insecurities; there will always be children and schools and the need to be educated. But what is education? It's not simply a question of assimilating facts and subject matter and acquiring skills. There are individual people emerging through those years from five to sixteen plus. How do we educate them? After they have left school and have gone out into the world, how will they educate themselves? Education is a lifelong process, and the arts have a great deal to do with it—whether we care to admit it or not.

Some of the greatest teachers I have known have been actors, dancers, musicians, and my grandma. I have learned more from a single performance by Galina Ulanova, Yehudi Menuhin, Maria Callas, Laurence Olivier, Peggy Ashcroft, John Gielgud, Uta Hagen, and many others than I ever learned from a whole course of study. And the reason is that each of these consummate artists brought a great talent and a lifetime of study and hard work to his or her performance. My grandma knew everything; she was simple and instinctive and very wise!

A child may not learn much about mathematics or irregular French verbs while watching *Androcles and the Lion,* but he will be curious about G. B. Shaw and his point of view, and the reading of the prefaces won't seem such a chore afterward because he will be curious. All good education is based on the need to know. That was my grandma's opinion.

Thought: What was I talking about? Oh yes, why I became a teacher!

Well, it never occurred to me that I could become an actress or a dancer or a designer and, least of all, a director. I saw myself only as a member of that other part of the theatre—the audience. It was only after years of study, following a strange path that was never clear to me at the time, that I finally found I had acquired most of the skills a director needs. After school I went to Goldsmiths College, London University, and at the same time studied modern dance and ballet. I was also interested in the visual arts, and so together with my musical education I was able to take on a job after graduation that involved a linked-arts program in an elementary school in London. Here I was able to apply immediately all that I was learning and at the same time work on my own skills. Those were the days when I left my house at 8:15 in the morning and seldom returned home before 11:30 at night, regularly, seven days a week.

Thought: I wonder where I got the energy and will power?

London in the 1950s and 1960s was an exciting place. There was so much theatre, dance, opera, music, and art, and, like many other young people, I was carried along by the force of it all and I saw everything I could. Somehow one always found the money; 2/6d got you into anywhere —$13^1/2$ new pence, or 20 cents! We did crazy things (we being a community of people of all ages who found one another in all the galleries and cheap seats of the West End), like seeing seventeen out of twenty-two performances, that the Bolshoi Ballet gave on their first visit to the West in 1957. Those were the days when a young man named Clive Barnes was selling a new publication called *Dance and Dancers* outside the gallery door of Covent Garden Opera House.

Classes, performances, theorizing, practicing, creating, experimenting, an endless pursuit of knowledge and ideas! And my children in school were the center of it all. I remember I tried to produce *The Blue Bird* with nine-year-olds and found the dialogue of that wonderful play just too much for them. After searching fruitlessly through Foyles's bookstore for suitable material, I came to the conclusion that I was going to have to sit down and write what I wanted, which I did. This was one of the most fruitful periods of my life. There was an immediate need and purpose for everything I did. I had to make my work work, and I had to organize every aspect of it. A good way to learn.

I have been asked many times why I never entered the mainstream of the regional repertory theatre, which is so good in Great Britain. That is the way most young aspiring directors go, in the hope that they will eventually make their way to the West End and, ultimately for a few, to fame and fortune.

It wasn't because I didn't want to deal with the competition. I always knew instinctively that it was children I wanted to work for but not in the usual, general sense of "children's theatre." I make no division of theatre into senior and junior leagues. There is only one kind of theatre for me, and it has to be good. Too often "children's theatre" is synonymous with second-rate. Only in countries like Russia, Poland, China, and Czechoslovakia are children's theatre and adult theatre considered of equal importance. It costs a lot of money to produce first-rate programs for anybody, and even enlightened countries like the U.S.A. with it's National Endowment for the Arts and Great Britain with its Arts Council can fund only so much when nuclear armament and space programs still have top priority in the national expenditure.

This is an old cry, far too familiar to raise any real response, but it is crucial. What has to happen to make those in power understand is not yet clear. Society everywhere is suffering from a lack of communication in a day and an age when the means to communicate are greater than ever before.

Thought: Something's wrong somewhere!

The history of civilization in all its various epochs and eras has relied on the creative artists of the time to relate an expression of their period. Could there be any doubt that the arts are essential?

I'm afraid so, especially now as we speed toward the twenty-first century. The most creative mass medium ever invented, television, has overtaken us. It is the greatest single educating and enlightening force in use all over the world, and the most powerful and, when in the right hands and the right minds, the most creative. But it has become the most abused. No other medium has taken such a beating within its comparatively short life-span, yet public and private concern do not seem to be able to change the direction that those in charge are hell-bent on pursuing.

Just think—it is possible, with international organization, to get in touch with 40 percent of the world's population at any given moment! For instance, more people watch one football game on American TV than go to all the theatres on Broadway in a whole season!

Thought: What is it about sports that draws such vast involvement when it is, for the most part, passive? Why do people come to be spectators at a physical event?

Certainly many more people are drawn toward sports than toward the arts. But isn't it all a form of theatre? The star performer can equally be the center forward in a football match just as much as the actor playing Hamlet.

Our theatres came from the ancient arenas and amphitheaters. Have we forgotten something in the last two thousand years? Perhaps it is because people can play the game themselves if they want to. There are certainly plenty of tennis courts, running tracks, swimming pools, and other sports facilities around. Maybe its the excitement that comes from keen competition and the money involved through prizes, betting, high wages for professional players, and profits made from the sales of goods. Or is it just a vicarious participation on the part of the spectator? The glory of the ancient gladiators has certainly fallen on the shoulders of the modern athlete. Is he or she the hero or heroine of our modern times? I have no answer to these questions, but I would like to pursue this point a little further.

At the beginning of a game nobody knows who will win, but each spectator has his own favorite team or player. He is involved for any number of reasons—and there is always the chance that something unexpected will happen. But at the beginning of a play often the events are far too predictable, the action is based on life, and we, the audience, may not want to identify with the conflicts and problems of the characters in front of us; they may seem too familiar.

But this is the very thing that makes theatre so exciting for me. I can go to see *King Lear* any number of times, know the play inside and out, and yet I am always appalled at the behavior of Goneril and Reagan, and I get so involved with that foolish old man Lear that I want to warn him of what is ahead. I care about him and his Fool. I don't particularly care about a star tennis player, yet these people are performers too, and they come under the same scrutiny as actors. The big difference between sports and the theatre is that one is totally designed and presented to create a given effect and the other is prepared, set up, and then let loose. Both require tremendous skill, technique, and personal commitment if they are to be first-rate. No game can be played stroke by stroke as a play is performed line by line, but there is a kind of theatre that has all the elements of sport, and that's my kind of theatre for children.

But I'm straying from the question.

Thought: Why do so many more people watch sports events than go to the theatre? Is it because we have made the arts elite and don't make them available to our children at an age when they can perhaps develop an interest?

Going to a theatre has a great social significance. You learn and accept certain conventions without question; the performers use speech, movement, dance, and singing to tell their stories. This is never questioned by adults.

One expects dancers not to talk—but why? Children are bound to ask, and I'm sure the simple answer of "Because they don't!" is perfectly acceptable.

Fact!

Another fact: Sitting in an auditorium with a lot of unfamiliar people who are all behaving in a particular way, is also a discipline a child respects. The "two-hour traffic of the stage," the intermissions, the foyer displays, refreshments, programs, dressing up to go in the first place, all make the ritual of the theatre an exciting and unusual event for a child. In a time when people are becoming more and more isolated and television is their main means of communication, we must encourage live happenings and performances. There is really no substitute for actually being there. No recording, whether film, video tape, or record album, can reproduce the *live* performance. So many other elements are necessary, too—the time, the place, and, most of all, the people, both artists and audience. The greatness of theatre is that it requires the coming together of all these elements to make it work. You and I are essential in this process. The writers, directors, composers, performers, and audience must all know something about human nature to understand the meaning of each presentation. Human beings is what it's all about! It's no good knowing what the rest of the world is doing if you don't know what is happening to your next-door neighbor!

Theatre encourages one to express an opinion. Language is necessary and words become very important when we try to explain why we did or did not like something we just saw. Somehow it matters more that you express yourself as you move out of your theatre seat and make your way home than it does when you turn off the TV switch and go to bed. Well, it does to me anyway!

It is pure joy to sit among an audience of children, whether it's watching *Peter Pan* in London, *The Nutcracker Suite* in New York, or a traditional play at the Central Children's Theatre in Moscow. The magical "if," the worlds of fantasy and imagination, are so easy for them to enter into, and the theatre simply helps them to realize some of their dreams. In almost every country in the world there is a traditional or classic theatre for children playing at some time of the year on high days and holy days—and, if you're lucky, season by season.

This is commercial or subsidized theatre, employing professionals where "the play's the thing." You pay your money and get your seat and usually make a social occasion out of your visit. I remember trying to persuade a group of fifteen-year-old boys—tough, likable, bright lads—to go to see the stage production of *Oh! What a Lovely War*. The piece was so dynamic and Joan Littlewood's production so brilliant that I wanted them to go. One adamantly refused even to consider it. His argument is worth remembering. First, he didn't know where it was, and a journey beyond the top of the road was like a voyage into the unknown. Second, it would cost money. It hadn't occured to him that it could be as cheap as the cinema or a football match. Third, he thought he had to dress up and eat after the show. "And I hold my knife and fork in the wrong hand!"

His presumption of required social graces, added to the fact that the idea of going to the theatre was not part of his family's life-style, might have kept him away forever if I hadn't pushed him a bit and persuaded him that he was as good as the rest of the audience. I told him about the groundlings in the time of Shakespeare, which gave him a point of reference. He decided to try it.

Years later I met him at the first night of a very serious play, and he told me that the theatre had become a part of his recreation. It remained different from anything else in his life, but he enjoyed it and so he continued to go.

The theatre is an institution and it is *there,* in all its various shapes and forms, whenever we want it, whether we go three times a week, twice a month, once a year, or never at all. We may have to travel to find it, the prices may increase, the quality may vary, but once we are addicted it's hard to kick the habit.

Now, even if we never set foot in a building called a theatre, there is a way drama can enter our lives on a regular basis.

Where? In school! How? Through the use of the technique of the actor, the director, and the playwright as applied to education.

Why? Well (long pause), we go to school for a minimum of eleven years, and somewhere in that span of time we are exposed to some, if not all, of the arts. There is almost certain to be a school play once a year or a concert on Speech Day. Some enterprising teacher will almost certainly organize an outing to the ballet or a professional production of one of the plays set for school examinations. I say this hopefully, as there are still many among us who do not believe that the arts are a valid teaching process or a valid learning experience for our children.

Thought: But what is school about and what are educators for? Preparing for life is my simple answer!

If drama is about life, about the way people behave and the things they do under certain circumstances and in specific situations, then the two things, education and drama, must come together. An adolescent girl has a much better chance of learning more about herself by watching Josie in Act 1 of *Epitaph for George Dillon* than by reluctantly listening to her parents nag her about the same problems. As well as the use of established plays, such as this, the methods and means of creating a role, interpreting a character, examining a situation, are all interesting and absorbing techniques of teaching.

Every good theatre director is usually a good teacher, and many teachers are exceptionally good actors. They are role playing the part of teacher!

When the director leads his company toward the realization of a play the production must be constructed in a way that can be repeated nightly and still carry the same interpretation. A great deal of discipline is required to make this happen.

The actor's discipline is equally demanding. It is a collaboration. You can't play a scene satisfactorily with another actor if he won't listen to you or look at you. Acting is a process of give and take—an essential lesson for us all to learn.

By the time I had finished college a new kind of educator had emerged, a professional in both education and the theatre, or education and movement or education and music, or arts and crafts. For most of us it was primarily an educational training. The ability to teach was the first requirement, and the acquisition of all the related skills one needed to direct and produce a play didn't happen while we were still students in college. These skills were going to take years to acquire in all sorts of places, with all kinds of teachers. Frequently one learned simply by trial and error, by being thrown in the deep end of a production knowing one had to meet a deadline.

Once I was assisting a very talented designer called Ronald Wilson at the Mercury Theatre in London. He was attempting to put a set together with little or no money for the famous Marie Rambert. Her reply to his appeal for cash I'll never forget. "Ronald, dear, I have no money. Make it out of brown paper." And we did. It looked terrific!

Thought: What was I talking about? Oh yes, the school play!

I was never interested in just putting on a play at the end of the term. I could never justify all those months of hard work for three nights of glory —if you were lucky! I know there are lots of commendable reasons for doing it, not the least of them being the cooperation and collaboration of all those taking part. But it needs a really experienced teacher to take charge and prevent the whole thing from becoming tedious and boring. I've done my fair share of such productions and I know from experience that its a big job to make it work the way it should if one isn't to do all the work one's self.

Frequently time is wasted, the children mess about a lot, they have fun, but as it is an after-school activity it does not have the same learning connotation as in-school courses.

Thought: Perhaps I'm being hard on the teachers. There are some very gifted, talented, persevering people in the profession who do a terrific job of producing *West Side Story* or *Guys and Dolls* or *The Wiz.* But there's more to it than that!

The real crux of the matter is that acting is a highly skilled and disciplined art. You can't just shove a script into someone's hands and tell him how to read it and where to move. That doesn't make sense, especially to the children. Recently I was working on a film that included six children. Their ages ranged from seven to twelve, and they were regular, everyday children, not the product of a drama school. The film, *Portrait of Grandpa Doc,* is about a family who spent their summers in a large wooden house on the New Jersey shore. That splendid actor Melvyn Douglas plays Grandpa Doc and the children play his grandchildren. During the filming a lovely relationship existed between them because he found time to answer their questions and tell them a bit about his early career. They had so many simple, direct questions to ask about their own characters, about previous circumstances that led up to their scenes, and their own motivations that had to be clearly explained to them. They were playing children of 1954, and as the oldest of them was born in 1964 it seemed like a neolithic age they had to relate to. Mr. Douglas spanned the years for them, and they listened to him and watched him at work with great interest and enjoyment. It was fascinating to observe them trying to figure out how his performance as Grandpa Doc was different from Mr. Douglas in real life.

I was fortunate to start work at a time when experimental techniques were not frowned on. I was not forced into a success/failure syndrome by having to produce results that indicated progress. By the 1950s the period of "free expression" was over but not the idea. It isn't enough to put on a record of *The Rite of Spring* and expect everyone to get up and dance! It's hard to interpret something through movement if you don't understand the imagery of the music and your body won't do what you want it to. It's rather like expecting someone to run the marathon before they've learned how to walk! And not all of us feel the need to express ourselves in an outward way.

Thought: Is everyone creative? I don't know! I have assumed on many occasions that they should be. Through my teaching and the operation of the Young People's Theatre, which I founded in New York at the City Center of Music and Drama in 1970, I have encouraged both adults and children to find pleasure and satisfaction in "doing" something imaginative and active.

But now that I think about it, it's rather like the character in Dickens who hands out the medicine with the unconvincing comment, "Take it; it's good for you!" Why? Because it says so on the bottle?

Some of us enjoy singing and dancing and acting. We all do it as small children, and some of us continue to do so all our lives, but most of us don't. We let something else do the work for us, and these days that seems to be one of the major functions of television. Let us suppose for a moment that all children are and want to be creative. How do they know it? How do they discover their potential for doing something that starts in the imagination and has no right or wrong way—just their way?

I once had a wonderful boy called Ronnie in one of my classes. He was thirteen years old and small for his age, but he had enormous energy. He had great trouble reading and writing, however, and he hated all aspects of formal education. Yet he was splendid in my classes. He had a rich imagination and he quickly realized the need for words when he wanted to explain his ideas, and his vocabulary extended because of his needs. One day, when he had done a particularly clever scene that had all the rest of the class in stitches, I asked him why he worked so well for me and not in his other lessons. His reply was simple: "Even when I try I can't read and I hate writin', but this is all about me and I'm good at it!"

I've often wondered what happened to that boy. Somebody told me he became a milk-delivery man. Well, his customers probably got the wrong change, but I'm sure they got a happy bottle of milk. Ronnie probably found all that improvising, role playing, and character study we did helped him deal with his daily customers. A unique milkman!

Thought: People. That's what its all about. People!

There are particular times in one's life when a certain group of people come together at a certain time. That's what happened at Markfield School, London N.15, in 1960. After I left Central School of Speech and Drama I was invited to start a drama department in this school, which had a student population of nine hundred ranging in age from twelve to seventeen years. It was a new school in a working-class neighborhood, with excellent facilities and more than its fair share of the problems that go with city life. I worked with all the students. Some had one session a week with me, and extra time was given to children with learning disabilities. At first there were two of us who had been specifically trained to do this work, and a third person came in later. We started with the real-life experiences of the children and tried to make them relate to their own behavior objectively. In view of the fact that all the shows they saw in the cinema and on the television were supposedly about people and the way they behave, we tried to bring them to a point of constructive criticism which then became a springboard.

We had to avoid the age-old problems of "I don't know what to say" and "I don't know what to do." We used all manner of things to stimulate them —scenes from plays, characters from popular books and TV series, lyrics from popular songs, incidents from the news, commercials, even poems. We found that plays of the Theatre of the Absurd fascinated them. The writings of Ionesco, Beckett, N. F. Simpson, and Kopit given in small doses stimulated incredible improvisations—and highly creative writing. The work spread from department to department. Gifted, energetic teachers in art, music, craft, woodwork, domestic science, needlework, graphic design, all undertook to work together, in the same way that different departments in a large resident theatre do. The work took on a greater meaning as it was explored. At the same time the work in the classroom sessions had developed so well that we wanted to share it with other people, so the Markfield Travelling Theatre was formed. Backed by a grant from the local council and encouraged by the principal of the school—an enlightened man— scripts were developed by the students and then every aspect of production undertaken by them to get the shows together. Under the direction of skilled and talented teachers, two- to three-week tours were undertaken twice a year to elementary schools in the district. In fact this was one of the first bus-and-truck companies made up entirely of school children. At Christmas and at the end of the summer term they played two performances a day of two productions—one for the infants five to seven and one for the juniors eight to fourteen. Everything technical was handled and managed by senior students, from set-up and lighting to the laundry. Big responsibilities for thirteen- and fourteen-year-olds, but it worked!

In the six years that I was there more than thirty productions emerged, and this was nothing compared to the work that was taking place in the classrooms with everybody all the time. The classroom was the foundation for all our work.

Thought: It wasn't all easy.

Now, looking back, it's hard to be totally objective or to remember correctly. There were rough times and tough times, but somehow the positive things have stayed in my mind. It was also a very exhausting period for me. I had done my first professional production as a co-director/adapter at the Mermaid Theatre and used a number of "my boys" in the cast. I had gone to Israel and directed and designed the same play, *Emil and the Detectives,* in Hebrew at the Habimah Theatre. In 1964 I took the Markfield Travelling Theatre to Czechoslovakia, where we played in Prague and did a tour of Bohemia. This was a fascinating experience. We had devised a program of action, mime, and movement with a strong British flavor, using as little language as possible but just enough that those with some knowledge of it could use.

Perhaps the most important happening of this period was the forming of a company called "Saturday Morning Theatre." I had been teaching for a number of years at a remarkable place called the City Literary Institute in Drury Lane. This school for adult studies had a strong theatre department that offered—and still does—professional training for the part-time student at reasonable prices. I held regular classes there about six times a week, in movement, mime, dance, and experimental-theatre techniques. Out of the hundreds of students who passed through my classes, a hard core of about twenty worked and trained with me for five years in the most committed and unselfish way. Sometimes we met for as many as twenty hours a week, and we regularly presented programs of original work in the small but pleasant theatre of the institute. We had presented a successful show at the Edinburgh Festival in 1962, and many people in both education and the theatre were taking notice of our work and it was receiving good press coverage.

I had had the beginnings of an idea in my mind for a long time concerning the amalgamation of the two forces in my life, the adults and the children. The big cinema distributors had established and maintained Saturday-morning cinema for years, and children turned up in droves. If a play was as accessible as a film, would they come? I again went to the local council, got another grant and the use of school halls on Saturday mornings—the latter being unheard of as far as school caretakers were concerned! I ventured forth with a company of forty into the *commedia dell' arte* —writing three plays in the traditional style, using my actors for the adult roles and the children for young members of the traveling *commedia* families. They were also our technical crew and stage managers.

The performances were free, and no one got paid. We used the school theatre facilities for set construction, for making the costumes, and for rehearsals. The productions looked good, the mixture of adults and children working together at the same level was very successful, and the children in the district came, saw, and had fun. I was warned that this would not happen, that no live performance would drag them out of the cinema; but the tours we had done with the Markfield Travelling Theatre paid off. The dividends were coming back! The same children were learning about choice, and given a choice, some of them chose to come to see a play instead of Walt Disney's latest film.

Thought: Why am I saying all this?

To underline the need for an alternative and to state categorically— again—that availability is at least half the battle! The other half is to make sure that what is presented is of fine quality, that there has been real consideration of the children and their environment, and that the effects of mass media on their minds and their attitudes have been carefully reviewed. Throughout this period we were working for high standards, with high energy, and for little or no money. A strong creative force carried us along, for all together we believed in what we were doing. We could see the results of it—in our audiences.

Now, you, dear reader, may be finding all of this rather diverse and rambling, but I had a purpose when I set out on this article, and that was to examine the question of children and theatre from my own childhood and from my personal teaching experience. I was now at a major point in my life, for it was from here on that I became a full-time professional. I left the secure world of regular employment for the razzmatazz of independent free-lancing, but all that had gone before, all those years of study and practice, of experimenting and producing, of setting impossible goals and somehow attaining them, all of this has been the firm basis of my work ever since. I believe in the arts and I believe in children; both are worth working for.

In the past twelve years I have worked in theatre, film, and television in numerous countries. I have traveled a great deal and been strongly influenced by places and people. Uta Hagen, both as a person and as an artist, has led me to understand aspects of theatre and acting that might otherwise have escaped me. It is a privilege to watch her at work both as an actress and as a teacher. It was because of her that I came to America in 1966 to join the faculty of the HB Studio in New York City, and I would have stayed if Professor Hugh Hunt had not offered me the Fellowship in Drama at Manchester University. I returned to England to take it up in 1966 and remained there for three years.

Thought: What do you do on a fellowship? Write a book usually!

Well, I didn't. Instead I worked out a method of using theatre techniques to aid the average teacher in the average classroom—a system I have refined over the years and still use today. It is a system that doesn't require a book to tell you page by page what you should, could, or ought to be doing but evolves a structure and a process of thinking that a teacher can immediately apply. The material the teacher needs is sitting in front of them—the children! I have done a lot of work in television with children, starting in 1964, using improvisational techniques. (I am fully aware that the word "improvisation" raises doubt in the minds of some who have been the victims of it when misapplied. It is an aspect of theatre that requires much skill and technique. Improvisation for me is a means to an end, not an end in itself.) The demands of time and space in the television studio had sharpened my sense of content and timing considerably. Now while on my fellowship I was able to combine all kinds of techniques with all kinds of needs, and slowly but surely the concept of the Young People's Theatre emerged. A university job has definite advantages: It allows you to work on your own but gives you the time to move around and search out other answers and alternatives. I traveled to Poland and Russia twice during this period.

The Central Children's Theatre in Moscow was a revelation to me, not specially for the productions it was presenting but for the operation of that large and exciting theatre. As with the Theatre of the Young Spectator in Leningrad, the directors were dedicated people with the means to do things we can only dream of. I learned much on my two theatrical visits there that has stood me in great stead ever since.

In 1967 I was invited back to Israel to the Habimah, and over a period of two years I had to learn how to cope with a state of war and still try to keep a semblance of regularity in my life. I directed a production of *The Fantasticks,* which was taken on a tour of the army camps from the Sinai Desert to the Kineret. This was an experience I wouldn't exchange for anything in the whole world. The magic of the theatre is so easy to recognize and so hard to explain, especially when you hear gunshots in the background and you still stay in your seats! One of the most important things an artist needs is encouragement from people who believe in what you are doing. Such a friend is Pearl Binder, an extraordinary woman. Writer, designer, illustrator, and a costume authority, she has helped me define some of my goals and get together the financial support for a workshop season under the auspices of the Royal Shakespeare Company. She has always had a clear picture of what the arts can do for each one of us, no matter what part of the social structure we represent. When I came back to America in 1970 she sent me on my way, hopeful that I would find support to keep my ideas alive and put them into practice. I was lucky. I did!

In 1970 the Young People's Theatre came into being at New York's City Center with the help and support of its then executive director, Norman Singer, a far-seeing and courageous human being. Using the concept of presentation/participation/realization I had worked on at Manchester University, I was able, over the next five years, to do a great deal of satisfying work. With a professional company of actors, in a wonderful space especially reconstructed for our use and a major grant from the Rockefeller Foundation, we presented forty-five theatre workshop productions. Thousands of children from all over New York City and New York State came to take part, and the theatre became established, firmly and happily.

But despite generous support from numerous and admirable foundations, the struggle to raise the cash we needed became too difficult, and the theatre had to close. However, the workers and the work remain. The need for the theatre has become greater even though the means to support it have become less. In the final analysis we must look at the age-old question: whose responsibility is it to fund the arts?

Thought: Where *does* the money come from to pay for it all?

To support artists and institutions, buildings, and year-round operations adequately—not extravagantly but adequately—a lot of money is needed. Does it come from taxes? Does it come from patrons of the arts? Does it come from commercial investment? From people and corporate structures looking for a tax shelter? Or from you and me and the general public, who understand and accept our own particular responsibility to the arts by paying for them?

A people and their culture are generally written down in history according to their achievements. In this respect the establishment of a national theatre is chicken feed compared with winning a war.

But we must be optimistic. Whatever happens, the joy and pleasure of the theatre will still be there in some form or other, and audiences will still find their way to the theatres, opera houses, concert halls, and auditoriums that continue to hold such fascination for so many of us.

Let them line up!

Let them fight for places!

And the younger the better!

Thought: This was really a very selfish way of writing an article!

PART V

Selected Bibliography

Broadman, Muriel. *Understanding Your Child's Entertainment,* New York: Harper & Row, 1977.

Chorpenning, Charlotte. *Twenty-One Years with Children's Theatre.* Anchorage, Kentucky: Anchorage Press, 1955.

Corey, Orlin. *Theatre for Children, Kid Stuff or Theatre?* Anchorage, Kentucky: Anchorage Press, 1974.

Courtney, Richard. *Play, Drama and Thought.* New York: Drama Book Specialists, 1974.

Davis, Jed, and Watkins, Mary Jane. *Children's Theatre.* New York: Harper & Row, 1961.

Donahue, John Clark. *The Cookie Jar & Other Plays.* Minneapolis: University of Minnesota Press, 1976.

Fisher, Caroline, and Robertson, Hazel. *Children and the Theatre.* Palo Alto: Stanford University Press, 1950.

Forkert, Maurice. *Children's Theatre That Captures Its Audience.* Chicago: Coach House Press, 1962.

Goldberg, Moses. *Children's Theatre: a Philosophy and a Method.* Englewood Cliffs, N.J.: Prentice-Hall, 1974.

Healy, Daty. *Dress the Shaw.* Rowayton, Conn.: New Plays, Inc., 1976.

Hodgson, John, and Richards, Ernest. *Improvisation.* London: Methuen, 1966.

Johnson, Richard. *Producing Plays for Children.* New York: Rosen Press, 1971.

Kase, Robert. *Children's Theatre Comes of Age.* New York: French, 1956.

Liften, Betty Jean. *Contemporary Children's Theatre* (plays). New York: Avon, 1974.

McCaslin, Nellie. *Children's Theatre in the United States: a History.* Norman, Oklahoma: University of Oklahoma Press, 1971.

Siks, Geraldine, and Dunnington, Hazel. *Children's Theatre and Creative Dramatics: Principles and Practices.* Seattle: University of Washington Press, 1961.

Swortzell, Lowell. *All the World's a Stage.* New York: Delacorte Press, 1972.

Way, Brian. *Development through Drama.* London: Longman, 1967.

Ward, Winifred. *Theatre for Children.* Anchorage, Kentucky: Anchorage Press, 1958.

Whitton, Pat Hale. *Participation Theatre for Young Audiences.* Rowayton, Conn.: New Plays, Inc., 1972.